Growing Vegetables California Style

by
Marsha Prillwitz

**illustrations and design by
Kathy Chillemi**

Poppy Press
P.O. Box 215485
Sacramento, California 95821
(916) 482-2119

Library of Congress Cataloging-in-Publication Data

Prillwitz, Marsha
Vegetable Gardening California Style
1.Vegetable gardening. 2.Container gardening.
I.Title

Library of Congress Card Catalog Number:
ISBN 0-9616145-0-1
Printed in the United States of America.
First printing in November, 1988.

CONTENTS

Part One: Garden Basics

Introduction v

Chapter One: Look Before You Leap 1
Time and Space, Sunlight, Water, Soil, Choosing the Crops, Planting Schemes, Keeping Track, Summary

Chapter Two: Care and Feeding of the Soil 13
Drainage, Soil Texture and Structure, Raised Beds, Amendments, Mulches and Fertilizers

Chapter Three: Insect- and Disease-Free Gardening 21
Weeds, Plant Diseases, Insects

Chapter Four: From Seed to Seedling to Garden Bed 31

Chapter Five: Container Growing 35

Part Two: The Vegetables 41

Cabbage, Broccoli, Brussels Sprouts, Cauliflower, and Turnips 45
Peppers 51
Tomatoes 57
Eggplant 65
Potatoes and Jerusalem Artichokes 69
Squash, Cucumbers, Melons and Pumpkins 75
Beans and Peanuts 83
Corn 91
Okra 97
Carrots and Parsnips 101
Beets, Spinach, and Swiss Chard 107
Radishes 113
Lettuce, Radicchio and other greens 119
Peas 125
Onions, Chives, Shallots, Garlic, and Leeks, ... 131

Appendices

A. Seed to Harvest Calender 136
B. Average and Record Frost Dates 139
C. Elevation and Normal Temperatures 140
D. University of California Cooperative Extension
   Offices 141

Index 142

Thanks

To Dave for your endless editing, computer
and business savvy, good humor, and
confidence.

To Jeremy for your patience and
encouragement.

To my family, friends, and faithful readers
who moved me to write this book.

Introduction

Gardening is one of the few things in life that is good for you and feels good too. The pleasure and pride of growing and eating your own produce easily outweighs the energy expended. But don't fool yourself into believing all you have to do is toss out the seeds and wait for them to produce. There is a certain amount of work involved. This book is dedicated to the recreational gardener who is willing to "get physical" in the garden, but doesn't plan to single-handedly carpet the whole planet with crops.

The seasons and daily weather patterns set the rhythm of our gardening activities. Well-seasoned gardeners learn to work within the confines of their local climatic conditions, observing and adjusting to Nature's patterns to increase their chances of a bountiful harvest. Fortunately, the clement climate of California is ideal for raising vegetables of all sorts, as long as the timing is right. This book is written primarily for California vegetable gardeners who live in the Central Valley and inland valleys of Northern and Southern California that experience hot, dry summers and mild, but pronounced winters. With minor variations, hillside gardeners can use the planting schedule, too. The map on the back cover shows this primary area in green.

Coastal, mountain, and desert gardeners can follow the general principles outlined in this book, but should check with their local cooperative extension offices for specific planting schedules. A list of these offices is in Appendix D.

The first section of this book will help you get started. Basic considerations of assessing the site, choosing crops, and drawing up a plan are covered in Chapter One. Chapter Two is devoted to the all-important garden medium, the soil. Horticultural habits to avoid insect and disease problems are discussed in Chapter Three. Starting your own plants from seed and growing vegetables in containers wraps up the first section of the book.

The second section provides specific information about the most popular garden crops. For each vegetable, you will find a brief history, cultural hints, particular insect and disease problems, and harvest and storage pointers.

The appendix includes a seed-to-harvest calender as well as California climatic information.

This book is intended to be used as a basic garden guide. Each garden has its own special conditions, each gardener has a distinct design or style in mind. In the garden you're free to experiment and try things your way. So relax and enjoy the new life soon to be sprouting up around you.

Part One - Garden Basics
Chapter One:
Look Before You Leap

Just how much space do you have to plant a garden? How much time do you have to spend? How much sunlight does the area receive? Is there an available source of water nearby? What is the condition of the soil? Can the gardener meet the plants' basic needs: air, water, nutrients, light, temperature and protection of their roots and foliage? These are the preliminary questions a new gardener should consider before plunging ahead full steam.

Time and Space

With careful planning, a very small amount of land, even a 10 foot by 10 foot plot, can yield a remarkable amount of tasty fresh produce. For a family of four, a well-managed 15 foot by 15 foot plot, as depicted on page two, can supply a good portion of the family's fresh vegetables year-round.

Starting small is a good idea, even if more space is available. That way, the gardener can gradually adjust work, social and leisure schedules to accommodate the new activity. In the spring when the soil needs to be tilled and readied for planting, the gardener needs to dedicate the most time to garden activities. During the summer, watering is the most time-demanding task. Weeding the beds will require some time, especially in the spring before the crops' canopy overshadows the weeds' growing grounds.

The gardener should count on touring the site daily, to mark the progress of the plants, check out the moisture of the soil, search for early signs of insects and diseases, pull a few weeds, and harvest mature crops. This is often more of a pleasure than a responsibility. Strolling through the garden after a hard day at work is a good way to unwind and shift gears.

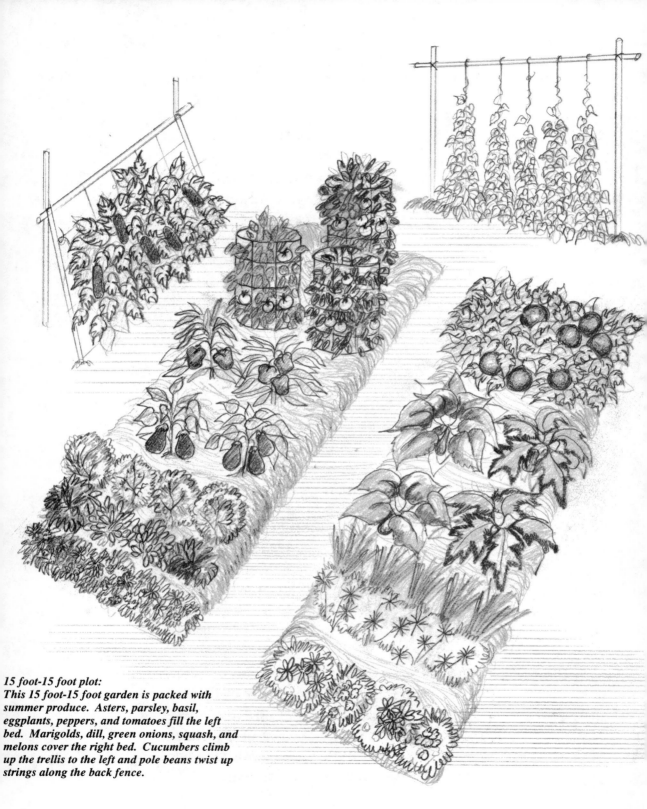

15 foot-15 foot plot:
This 15 foot-15 foot garden is packed with
summer produce. Asters, parsley, basil,
eggplants, peppers, and tomatoes fill the left
bed. Marigolds, dill, green onions, squash, and
melons cover the right bed. Cucumbers climb
up the trellis to the left and pole beans twist up
strings along the back fence.

Experienced gardeners, as well as novices, should consider the amount of land they can manage comfortably each year before marking off the plot. Many a garden has been abandoned long before harvest time due to an over-enthusiatic beginning.

Like weekend athletes after their first game of the season, weekend gardeners, too, experience their share of aches and pains after their first big day in the garden. Ten to fifteen minutes of simple stretching exercises to warm up before gardening will help to lessen the Monday morning moans and groans.

Sunlight

Six hours of direct sunlight is the minimal requirement for most garden vegetables. As long as they are planted during the proper season, too much sun will never be a problem. Trees and shrubs not only shade out the sun, but also draw water and nutrients away from the vegetable garden. If possible, do not situate your plot within 20 feet of shallow-rooted trees or shrubs. The benefit of fruit and shade trees cannot be overlooked, however, so be willing to compromise if the situation calls for it. Partially shaded tomato plants may not produce as well as the neighbor's full sun counterparts, but when the sun-robbing plums are ready for harvest, slightly reduced tomato production doesn't matter as much.

Shade tolerance is relative to the amount of light and the amount of warmth the plant receives. Thus, plants in warm and shady areas fare better than those in cool and shady areas. Vegetable seed will germinate slower in a shady bed and the plant will take longer to mature, so plant shaded vegetables a little later in the season, when the ground has warmed. Once the plant has matured, light exposure can beincreased by staking and trellising. This will raise the plant toward the sun. Leafy vegetables such as lettuce, kale, spinach, cabbage, and mustard tend to accept more shade. Beets, cucumbers, peas, onions, broccoli, carrots, radishes, and most herbs will also succeed in partial shade conditions. Avoid planting sun-loving eggplants, melons, squash, peppers or corn in heavy shade.

Water

A convenient watering system will save the gardener time and aggravation beyond measure. The system you choose will depend upon the amount of land under cultivation, the types of crops planted, and how much money you have to spend.

For a small, compact garden, regular lawn sprinklers or furrow irrigation will do the job. As the garden expands and watering becomes more of a burden, soaker hoses, drip irrigation systems or permanent sprinkling systems may be called into service. Often times, sprinklers and soaker hoses interconnected with a Y-valve can accommodate the average home garden plot.

Whatever system the gardener chooses, the amount of water and the frequency of irrigation will be the most important variables. The general rule is to water early in the day, deeply, thoroughly, and regularly yet infrequently. The temperature, wind, sun intensity, humidity, the soil's water holding capacity, and the variety of plants grown will determine the actual watering schedule. 1 1/4 to 1 1/2 inches of water every seven to eight days is usually about right.

Periodically digging into the soil with a trowel to see how deeply the water has penetrated will help the gardener gauge whether the amount and frequency of irrigation is correct.

The plants themselves will demonstrate lack of water by wilting, yellowing, or drying out. For example, wilted squash leaves are common on hot afternoons, but if they are wilted in the morning, it is a sign that more water is needed.

Soil

Since plants obtain the majority of their water, air, and nutrients through their roots, you will want to be particularly observant of the soil. Fortunately, with time and effort the soil can be improved. Chapter Two will deal with assessing and improving the soil's fertility, texture, and structure.

When choosing a site, the first thing to look for in regard to the soil is the degree of slope and drainage. A slight slope is fine, as long as the gardener is aware of it and designs the beds or rows to run across rather than up and down the slope.

Special trellising or other structural bolstering is often required for gardens in hilly areas to control erosion.

If water tends to puddle up on top of the soil rather than filter freely through the soil, drainage may be a problem. The addition of organic matter and cultivation of raised beds can help remedy bad drainage. These techniques, too, will be discussed in Chapter Two.

In order to reduce worries later on in the season, it helps to weed the bed thoroughly before cultivating the soil. After waiting two weeks for a new crop of weed seedlings to sprout, reweed the bed, then plant. Catching any new weeds before they go to seed will keep future generations under control.

Once the bed is cleared of weeds and debris, and is dry enough to work, the soil can be tilled. Usually this can be done by hand with a good spade. The soil should be turned and loosened to a depth of six to eight inches for most crops, 12-18 inches for cucumbers, squash, melons, and root crops.

Choosing the Crops

The first thing to do in January is make up a list of all the vegetables you want to grow that year. Then break down the list into warm-season and cool-season crops.

Cool-season crops are those in which the edible part is a root, stem, leaf or immature flower part. Generally these can be planted in early spring, late summer, or fall. Some cool-season crops are lettuces, greens, cabbages, turnips, beets, peas, onions, broccoli, cauliflower, Brussels sprouts, and carrots.

With warm-season crops, the edible part of the plant is the fruit. Such crops as tomatoes, peppers, eggplant, beans, corn and okra fit into this category.

Each plant has different temperature and day length requirements which determine germination, growth, and fruit production. Some crops are more flexible than others. The second section of this book will give you specific information on each vegetable.

After breaking down the list into warm-season and cool-season crops, the gardener should seriously consider how much the family will eat, freeze, can, or peddle, and about how much space is available.

Some plants require much less space than others. The use of trellises, "gro-nets" and other supports to encourage plants to grow up, rather than sprawl over the garden bed, can allow the limited-space gardener to grow some of the bed-hogging plants.

Space saving crops	Space demanding crops
peppers	corn
eggplant	squash
beans	tomatoes
beets	cucumbers
radishes	melons
lettuces	
cabbage, broccoli, cauliflower	

After taking space, time and appetites into account, it's time to start shopping for seeds. Many excellent seed varieties and convenient transplants are available from local nurseries. However, if you want a special variety, or just want to see what is available in the realm of vegetables, these nine seed catalogs are geared toward the home vegetable gardener:

W. Atlee Burpee
300 Park Ave.
Warminster, Pa. 18974
215 674-4915

Gurney Seed and Nursery
Yankton, S.D. 57079
605 665-1930

Johnny's Selected Seeds
Foss Hill Road
Albion, Maine 04910
207 437-9294

Le Marche Seeds Intl.
P.O. Box 566
Dixon, Ca. 95620
($2.00)
916 678-9244

Nichols Herb and Rare
   Seeds
1190 North Pacific Hwy.
Albany, Oregon 97321
503 928-9280

Redwood City Seed Co.
P.O. Box 361
Redwood City, Ca. 94064
($.50)
415 325-7333

Park Seed
Cokesbury Road
Greenwood, S.C.
29647-0001
803 223-7333

Shepherd's Garden Seeds
7389 West Zayante Rd.
Felton, Ca. 95018
($1)
408 335-5400

Vermont Bean Seed Co.
Garden Lane
Bomoseen, Vt. 05732
802 265-4212

It's a good idea to order all of these catalogs and have them on hand.

Shopping through the catalogs provides the gardener with more comprehensive varietal information. You will find that some varieties of plants have been developed to resist diseases or pests. Others have been adapted to resist heat, drought, or climatic conditions. Bush, dwarf and "mini" varieties are available for many crops that could not otherwise have been grown in smaller plots or container gardens.

Seed catalogs often note the distinctive taste of each variety, its storability, size, the number of days to maturity, and whether it is determinant or indeterminant. A determinant plant produces all its fruits during one short period, while an indeterminant plant has a longer harvest period. For example, with a determinant tomato plant, all the tomatoes ripen within two weeks. If you are growing tomatoes for canning, this is great. However, if you want to harvest them throughout the summer for salads, you would want to select an indeterminant variety.

When choosing vegetable seeds, locally adapted varieties, typically ones that the neighbors have grown successfully for years, are the best bet. Trying new or exotic old varieties, in addition to the regulars, can be fun and pleasantly surprising. It's a good idea to plant new additions next to tried-and-true varieties in order to make valid comparisons.

Planting Schemes

As a final reality check on your vegetable wish list, chart out the planting scheme on paper. North to south running rows are usually the best, with taller plants like corn planted on the north end so they don't shade out their shorter bed-mates. The mature size of the plants should be considered when spacing them. If possible, plant crops with similar growing periods in the same area.

Slow growers	Speedy crops
tomatoes, peppers, eggplant	cabbage family
corn	beans, peas
onions	lettuce, greens
okra	radishes
squash, melons, cucumbers	carrots
pumpkins	

Crop rotation, succession planting, relays, intercropping and companion planting are variations of planting schemes. These schemes can help the gardener increase production, maintain good soil conditions, lengthen harvest periods, and reduce insect and disease problems.

The main point of *crop rotation* is to follow heavy feeding plants with light feeders or soil builders. Cabbage family crops, corn, beets, cucumbers, eggplant, okra, pumpkin, spinach, squash, sunflowers, tomatoes, and watermelons are heavy feeders. These crops should be followed by light feeders such as peppers, onions, carrots, parsnips, potatoes, chard or turnips, or by the soil builders - clover, peas, beans or peanuts.

Through crop rotation the gardener can avoid consecutive plantings of crops which are susceptible to the same diseases or insect pests. Generally, related vegetables are vulnerable to the same problems. The main garden families are: Cucurbitaceae - cucumbers, melons, squash, and pumpkins; Leguminosae - beans, peas, and peanuts; Cruciferae - cabbage, broccoli, Brussels sprouts, cauliflower, radishes and turnips, and Solanaceae - tomatoes, peppers, eggplant and potatoes.

Succession planting entails planting a later crop as soon as you take out an early one, all in the same season. Usually the first crop is a fast maturing light feeder, the succeeding crop being a medium to slow maturing one. Some typical successions are spinach then beans, broccoli then corn, and peas then peppers.

Instead of replacing one crop with another like succession planting, *relays* are successive planting of the same crops. For instance, the gardener plants one block of corn the first week, then another the next week and yet another the next. Peas, beans, corn, carrots and onions are often planted in relays to stagger the harvest.

The practice of mixing more than one crop in the same bed is called *intercropping*. Quick maturing crops can be harvested and removed, making room for the larger, slower

9

maturing crops planted at the same time. Radishes, green onions, leaf lettuce and carrots are good fast-maturing inter-croppers.

Companion planting is the art of growing compatible plants near each other, often to the benefit of both. Rodale Press is most often quoted in this area.

Keeping Track

Any planting strategy requires a good basic garden plan and a simple record of each year's crops. Keeping track of the garden on paper enables the gardener to practice crop rotation more effectively, to determine the success of different varieties, to better control pest problems, to calculate the best planting schedules, and to anticipate harvest time and estimate economic benefits.

The first step is to chart out the garden space. Use 8 1/2 inch by 11 inch paper or graph paper and make several copies of the master diagram to use in subsequent seasons. This visual representation will serve as a valuable reference for crop rotations and will help you picture a reasonable spacing scheme. For each major planting, fill in a new diagram, noting the date on each new sheet. A summary of the season may be useful for future reference.

More detailed, dated entries will provide specific data which will make the journal most valuable. Record all key activities or observations. Enter notes describing daily actions and conditions, such as:

- First rain of the season, last rain of the season
- Last spring frost, first winter frost
- Preparation of the bed: digging, weeding, irrigation practices
- Amendments to the soil: what was added, when and how much
- Varieties of crops planted: when planted, where purchased

- First signs of problems: insects, diseases, weeds
- Methods of control practiced: successes and failures
- Unusual weather conditions: temperature and moisture
- Harvest: dates, amounts, taste and quality of vegetables.

Keep the entries short, but personal. Note all plantings on your master diagram.

An optional but interesting section of the garden journal is the financial page. Although most people receive ample satisfaction from the harvest alone, an account of investments and gains may be revealing, gratifying and even necessary during hard economic times.

One page would be devoted to investments, another to gains. For the investments sheet, set up columns for the date, item purchased, price, and a running total. You don't need to be too specific here. The conscientious consumer may decide to save receipts and empty seed packages in the notebook or toss them into a shoe box.

The profit sheet is less concrete. Although it's difficult to calculate the value of home-grown harvest, an estimate of the number or pounds of vegetables produced and an approximate market value is relatively easy and quite rewarding.

By the end of the season, the investment sheet and the profit sheet can be totalled up and compared. This may help you decide what to plant next year.

Summary

In short, you can grow a productive vegetable garden if you remember these Ten Tips capsulated from Chapter One:

1. Start small. A 15-foot by 15-foot area should suffice.
2. Allow enough time for spring tilling, regular watering, and daily garden tours.
3. Make sure the site receives at least six hours of direct sunlight each day, and avoid shade and root competition.
4. Secure a water source and design an irrigation plan. Water early, deeply, thoroughly, regularly, but infrequently.
5. Choose a slopeless site with good drainage.
6. Remove as many weeds as possible before planting, and eliminate new weeds before they go to seed.
7. Cultivate the soil to a depth of at least six to eight inches, 12 to 18 inches for deep-rooted plants.
8. Select vegetables that you enjoy eating, that fit into the garden space, and that are well adapted to the local climate.
9. Chart out the garden on paper before planting; keep written records for your own information and convenience.
10. Plant during the proper season.

Chapter Two:
Care And Feeding Of The Soil

Nature restores and replenishes the soil through an ongoing cycle of growth and decomposition. As old plants die and decay, they eventually return to the soil to nourish new plants. By supplementing this natural process, the gardener can modify or maintain the garden soil so it can support more intensive production. This chapter will take you through the world of soil drainage, soil texture and stucture, amendments, mulches and fertilizers, and soil acidity-alkalinity (pH.)

Drainage

How fast or slow water moves through the soil is a measurement of its drainage. Sandy soils usually drain very quickly while clay soils are slow drainers.

To check your soil's drainage, dig a hole two feet deep. Fill it with water and let it set for a day. Then fill it again. If the water level drops more slowly than 1/4 inch in an hour, you have poor drainage. Excellent drainage is evident if the water level drops faster than one inch per hour.

Soil TextureAnd Structure

A good farmer can tell the value of a soil by picking up a handful, feeling it, smelling it, and checking its color. We city gardeners can learn about our garden soil by following the farmer's example. Pick up a handful of soil and rub it between your hands. If it feels scratchy or gritty and crumbles easily, you have a sandy soil. Clay soils will feel slippery and sticky when wet, and hard when dry. Silty soils fall between sand and clay, feeling smooth and slippery when wet, but not sticky.

A balanced combination of different textures, known as loams, are the easiest to handle and the most productive garden soils. Heavy clay soils with little organic matter are the most difficult to work.

For a more graphic display of the proportions of clay, silt, and sand in the soil, try the old jar method. Fill a quart jar two-thirds with water and then add soil until the jar is nearly full. Screw on the lid and shake vigorously. Let the soil settle for a few hours. You should end up with a layer of sand on the bottom, silt in the middle, and clay on the top.

Cultivation, irrigation, and fertilization practices are determined in part by soil texture. A comparison of sand and clay soil textures will illustrate this point:

SAND:	*CLAY:*
• Large particle size	• Fine particle size
• Quartz is major component	• Product of weathered rock
• Drains rapidly	• Drains slowly
• Light soil, warms up fast	• Heavy soil, will crust over
• Tends to be acidic	• Basic or neutral pH
• Rapid leaching of nutrients	• Will hold nutrients
• Poor water holding capacity	• Four to five times better water-holding capacity than sand.

Along valley floors, near rivers and former river pathways, the coarser sandy soils prevail. The further removed from the stream beds, the finer clay soils dominate.

The presence of hardpan is a common condition. Chemical leaching can form an impenetrable layer of soil which, if it forms within two to three feet of the surface, can restrict the growth of plants. The formation of such a barrier occurs when rain moves minerals to a certain depth where they are then chemically bonded together.

Similarly, a compacted layer of the soil occurs most often

with the use of heavy machinery. On a smaller scale, the trails of an enthusiastic gardener through the vegetable bed can also cause mechanical soil compaction.

For small areas, adding organic matter and raising the beds of flowers and vegetables may be all that is needed. Breaking through the hardpan layer directly beneath new plantings of trees or shrubs will allow roots and water to pass through it.

In addition to alleviating hardpan woes, increased organic matter and raised bed gardening can help improve soil structure. Groupings or "aggregates" of soil particles are held together by small bits of clay and organic matter. The size and form of these aggregates determine soil structure. A "granular" structure, one with large pores between aggregates which lets roots "breathe" and grow and lets water drain through easily, is ideal for plant growth. A "massive" soil structure, one in which soil particles are packed closely together, is a poor environment for plants because there is no room for air, water or roots.

To avoid soil structure breakdown from a granular to a massive state, avoid cultivating the soil when it is too wet or too dry; add organic matter, and avoid compaction.

Soil Amendments, Mulches, and Fertilizers

Amendments are applied to improve the structure or texture of the soil. Organic matter is the primary category of soil amendments. The content of organic matter differs greatly from soil to soil. Sacramento Silty Clay contains five percent organic matter, Yolo Loam a mere one percent, while Venice Peaty Muck boasts 60 percent organic matter. In places with hot, dry summers, organic matter breaks down very rapidly and needs to be replenished regularly.

When added to sandy soils, organic matter helps hold moisture and nutrients in the root zone. Large quantities of organic matter will also improve the air circulation of a clay soil. Some popular organic soil amendments are compost, manure, shredded or ground bark, peat moss, rice hulls, and sawdust.

The composting process converts raw organic matter to a soil-like substance through the heat of the compost pile. When added to the soil, compost improves its texture and structure.

Common compost materials are alfalfa, bloodmeal, bone-meal, garden residues, grass clippings, kitchen garbage, leaves, manure, peat moss, rice hulls, and straw. Chop up large materials before using them and avoid using meat scraps which attract flies and rodents. Here is one way to build a compost pile:

Traditional compost pile:
• layer of organic matter
• thin layer of soil every one to 1 1/2 feet
• layer of organic matter
• thin layer of ammonium sulfate, manure, or other Nitrogen source
• layer of organic matter
Build layers until the pile is 3 feet wide and 4 to 5 feet tall. Water pile every 4-5 days during the summer. Cover to protect from excessive rain during the winter. Turn the pile every 4 weeks. Compost will be ready in 3 months.

You can find a source of commercial compo
amendments in the Yellow Pages under "Sand an

The amount of amendments added must be ϵ
physically alter the structure of the soil. Usually one
one half of the final mix should be amendment. Thus,
intend to improve the top 12 inches of soil, you'll need ι
four to six inches of organic matter or other amendment

Mulches differ from amendments in that they are applied
top of the bed, not worked into it. Wood chips, bark, and gra
clippings are common mulch materials. They benefit the garden by:

- maintaining soil structure and preventing crusting,
- decreasing water loss from the soil surface,
- increasing air to the roots and soil organisms,
- moderating soil temperature,
- helping with weed control, and
- reducing soil compaction from water and traffic.

A summertime mulch is especially valuable as a heat re-
ducer and water saver. To be effective as a weed controller, the
layer of mulch needs to be six inches deep.

Fertilizers differ from amendments and mulches in that
their main function is to provide plant nutrients, not to improve soil structure. Organic amendments and mulches, however, do provide small amounts of nutrients to the plants.
Bonemeal, bloodmeal, cottonseed meal, fish emulsion, and
seaweed extract are other forms of organic fertilizers.

Synthetic fertilizers are more concentrated and faster acting
than their organic counterparts. There are many synthetic fertilizers available, each with specific properties and purposes.
Read the package label carefully to avoid fertilizer burn to the
plants. If the lable reads 5-10-20, that means that particular
bag of fertilizer contains five percent nitrogen (N), ten percent
phosphorus (P), and 20 percent potassium (K).

It is seldom necessary to fertilize for the minor elements

required by plants. Potassium, sulfur, calcium, and magnesium are rarely lacking in home garden soils in California. Most soils in this state are naturally low in nitrogen, and many weathered hardpan soils in the foothills may be low in phosphorus.

Nitrogen is easily filtered down through the soil whereas phosphorus and potassium are practically immobile. Therefore, phosphorus and potassium can be worked into the soil once during a growing season, before planting, while nitrogen is often added periodically as the plants mature.

Soil acidity-alkalinity, often referred to as pH, is a number from zero to 14. Below seven indicates an acidic (sour) soil; above seven, an alkaline soil; and exactly seven is a neutral or sweet soil. Most plants prefer a slightly acidic soil. To make soil more acidic, an application of ammonium sulfate, aluminum sulfate, or sulfur is usually recommended. To make soil less acidic, add lime to the soil. This is rarely needed.

Raised Beds

Using raised beds can help the gardener improve soil structure and overcome hardpan problems. Raising the beds can also remedy poor drainage and waterlogged soils. Soils in a raised bed will warm up earlier in the spring, giving the gardener a head start over the neighbors. Finally, cultivating raised beds will provide convenience for the gardener who has trouble bending over or kneeling.

The size and shape of the beds can be adjusted to meet your own needs. A raised bed is usually four to five feet wide so its center can be reached easily from either side.

The main idea behind raising a bed is that the growing surface ends up higher than surrounding soil surface. A bed is "raised" by cultivating the soil to increase air space, and by adding organic matter.

Raised beds can be free standing or enclosed with structured sides composed of wood slats, bricks or other building material. Beds with perennial crops such as strawberries and asparagus are often enclosed, while beds that are frequently cultivated are left open, without sides, for easier digging.

Before you begin digging, make sure the soil is dry enough.

Working the soil when it is too wet can damage its structure. A handful of soil that falls apart after being squeezed together into a ball, rather than sticking to your hands, is dry enough to be spaded or tilled. If in doubt, wait.

Most home gardens can be dug by hand. A short handled, flat-edged spade and a short handled fork are the best tools for raised bed preparation.

Here is how to prepare a raised bed:

1. Mark off the length and width of the bed.
2. Remove weeds and other debris.
3. Dig out a trench across the width of the bed about one foot deep and one foot wide.
4. Move the soil from this trench to the far end of the bed.
5. To "double dig" the bed for crops such as cucumbers and squash with deep diving roots, loosen soil beneath the trench another 6-12 inches.
6. Apply a layer of organic matter and fertilizer as desired on top of the bed.
7. Standing on the entrenched portion of the bed, dig a second trench, loosening the soil, then throwing it forward into the first trench.
8. Work backwards, toward the end of the bed, stopping frequently to rake smooth the completed portions.
9. Fill in the trench left at the end of the bed with the soil moved from the front of the bed.

Chapter Three:
Insect- And Disease-Free Gardening

In the garden, the interrelationship of plants, soil, water, air, insects and other living things (including the gardener) determines crop health. Careful observation and simple manipulation of the garden ecology can minimize problems.

If the gardener follows the Ten Tips listed in Chapter One plus these common-sense management practices, many garden ills can be prevented.

1. Maintain rich, fertile, well-drained soil to promote plant health, rapid growth, and decreased susceptibility to diseases and insects.
2. Diversify plantings and practice crop rotation to reduce losses. This will discourage crop-specific insects and diseases.
3. Select disease-resistant and insect-resistant varieties of plants or seeds.
4. Use cages, trellises, nets or stakes to keep vegetables up off the ground.

Weeds

Those prolific plants we call "weeds" are impossible to eliminate, but can be controlled. They produce countless seeds, thrive in drought or wet conditions, and survive the worst of soils. Because weeds compete with crops for light, nutrients, and water and because they harbour insects and diseases, the gardener is wise to keep their numbers down.

Physical controls include uprooting, hoeing, burying, cutting, smothering, burning, and mowing. Chemical controls, herbicides, can be difficult to apply and are seldom necessary in the home garden situation.

Annual weeds-- those that germinate, flower, go to seed and

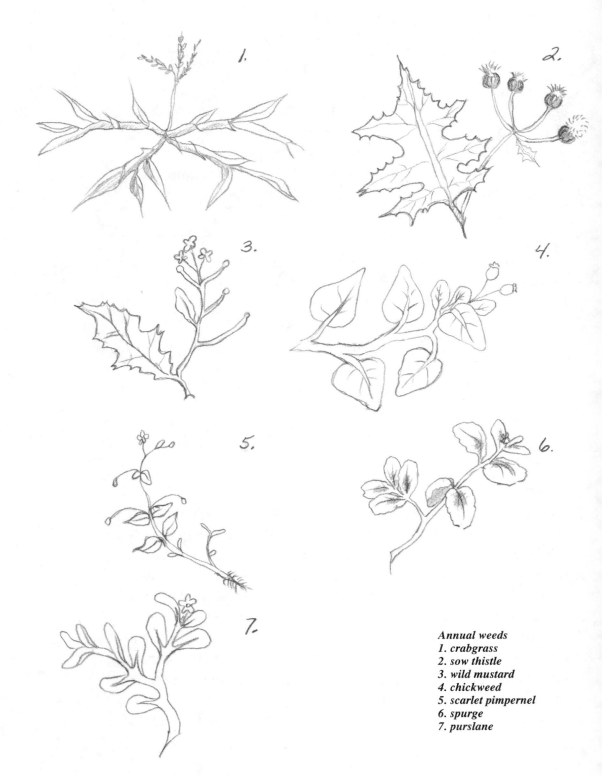

Annual weeds
1. crabgrass
2. sow thistle
3. wild mustard
4. chickweed
5. scarlet pimpernel
6. spurge
7. purslane

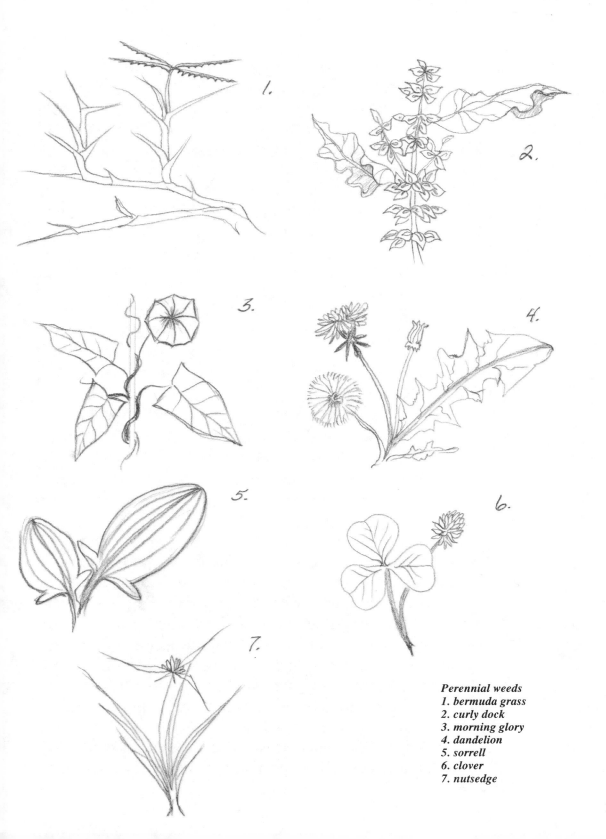

Perennial weeds
1. *bermuda grass*
2. *curly dock*
3. *morning glory*
4. *dandelion*
5. *sorrell*
6. *clover*
7. *nutsedge*

23

die in one year-- are easier to control than perennials which spread underground as well as by seed. Annual weeds include crabgrass, barnyard grass, mustard, sowthistle, pineapple weed, cheeseweed, chickweed, scarlet pimpernel, broadleaf filaree, and spurge. Some perennial weeds are bermuda grass, dallis grass, curly dock, morning glory, dandelion, sorrell, clover and nutsedge.

These simple practices will eventually reduce the number of weeds to a manageable level:

1. Remove weeds when they first appear, before they go to seed.
2. Maintain a mulch at least six inches deep to discourage new weeds.
3. Learn to identify weeds and become familiar with their life cycles to disrupt their growth at the optimal time.
4. Remove as many weeds as possible before planting a new bed. After a crop of remaining weed seeds germinates, (usually within two weeks) repeat the process before planting.

Plant Diseases

The technical definition of a plant disease, or pathogen, is "an injurious disturbance in form or function in a plant resulting from a continuous irritation." In plain English, a plant disease is anything that harms a plant after pestering it for some time. Infectious diseases-bacteria, fungi and viruses-spread from plant to plant. Less obvious, non-infectious diseases result from environmental conditions. Physical injuries, nutritional deficiencies, pollution, and exposure to toxic materials are non-infectious diseases.

In order for any plant disease to become established, three interrelated and equally important requirements must be met:

1. Presence of the causal agent (the pathogen-bacteria, fungi, etc.)
2. Suscept (plant in weakened, susceptible state)
3. Environment favorable to establishment of disease (temperature, moisture).

The *sign* of a disease is evidence of the pathogen itself while a *symptom* is the visible effect of the pathogen upon the plant, such as yellowed leaves or stunting. Chemical control of pathogens in the home garden is limited. The following cultural practices are the best remedies for preventing diseases:

---

1. Keep out of the garden when it is wet.
2. Remove diseased plants as soon as possible. Do not use them in compost.
3. If you smoke, do not touch tomato, eggplant, pepper or potato plants to avoid spreading mosaic virus.
4. Use mulches to maintain uniform moisture, thus controlling fruit rots and blossom end rot.
5. Control insects, such as aphids, thrips and leafhoppers, which often transmit diseases.

Insects

One of the most heartbreaking experiences of gardening is having one's carefully nurtured plants done in by an insect attack. In many cases, the battle of the bug is a losing venture for the gardener. Fortunately, in a diversified garden, the natural balance of predator/prey usually keeps the numbers of destructive insects under control.

To give nature a helping hand, follow these preventive cultural practices:

1. Spade the soil regularly to increase air space, improve structure, and destroy eggs and larvae of some insects.
2. Keep a tidy garden, removing diseased or dead fruit and vegetables and discarding any debris which may provide a home for insects.
3. Learn to tolerate some damage.
4. If damage is unacceptable, carefully identify causes first, then move to remedies.
5. Begin with the least generally destructive and most insect specific controls. For example, hand-picking, physical barriers, water spraying, and biological controls should be considered before resorting to chemical methods.
6. Learn to identify and protect beneficial insects. See Page 30, for some of the good ones.

Most insects feed at night rather than during the heat of the day. A midnight insect patrol can shed a lot of light on which critters are actually causing damage. Take a flashlight along and be prepared to stomp those hungry destroyers.

Insects are often broken into two general classifications based upon the kind of damage they cause. "Sucking insects" cause bleached, yellow, or strippled leaves while "chewing insects" actually bite away portions of the leaves or other plant parts. Aphids, Harlequin bugs, stink bugs, leafhoppers, mites, thrips, and whiteflies are sucking insects. Some examples of chewing insects are beetles, caterpillars, cabbage worms, cabbage loopers, cutworms, tomato hornworms, corn earworms, earwigs, sowbugs, grasshoppers, crickets, and leaf miners.

Bacillus thuringiensis (B.t.) which is sold as Dipel, Vegetable and Insect Attack, or Safer's Caterpillar Killer is a biological insecticide effective against worms and caterpillars. It is harmless to all other forms of life. Pulverized flowers of a chrysanthemum are used to manufacture pyrethrum, an insecticide toxic to aphids, white flies and leafhoppers. Traps baited with a pheromone, a strong sex lure or a food lure have been developed for some moths and beetles. Nontoxic yellow bars covered with a sticky substance trap many flying insects. Leafhoppers, Mexican bean beetles, leaf miners, and white flies are some of the insects that are lured to their deaths by their love of bright yellow colors.

If a gardener has tried cultural and biological controls and decides that a chemical control is warranted, the least toxic chemical should be used first. Strict adherence to label instructions and precise record keeping of applications are important. The gardener should be protected from contact or inhalation, store the products out of the reach of children and pets, and dispose of the containers safely. Last but not least, consider the effects of the pesticide on the environment: air, water, soil, and beneficial insects and animals.

The three main chemical insecticides commonly used in the vegetable garden are malathion, carbaryl, and diazanon. Malathion is the most popular and versatile synthetic insecticide. It can be used against most sucking insects. Carbaryl, which is sold as Sevin, is relatively safe for humans, but is toxic to bees and encourages mite infestations. Diazinon is more toxic than Malathion or Sevin. It is often used as a pre-plant soil treatment for control of a wide range of insects.

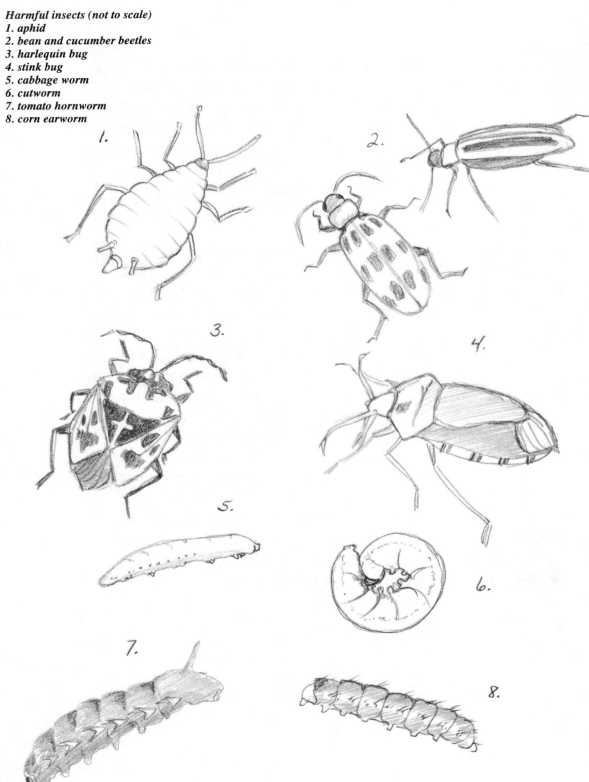

Harmful insects (not to scale)
1. aphid
2. bean and cucumber beetles
3. harlequin bug
4. stink bug
5. cabbage worm
6. cutworm
7. tomato hornworm
8. corn earworm

1.

2.

3.

4.

5.

6.

7.

8.

28

9. earwig
10. grasshopper
11. cricket
12. leaf miner
13. mite
14. squash vine borer
15. thrip
16. whitefly

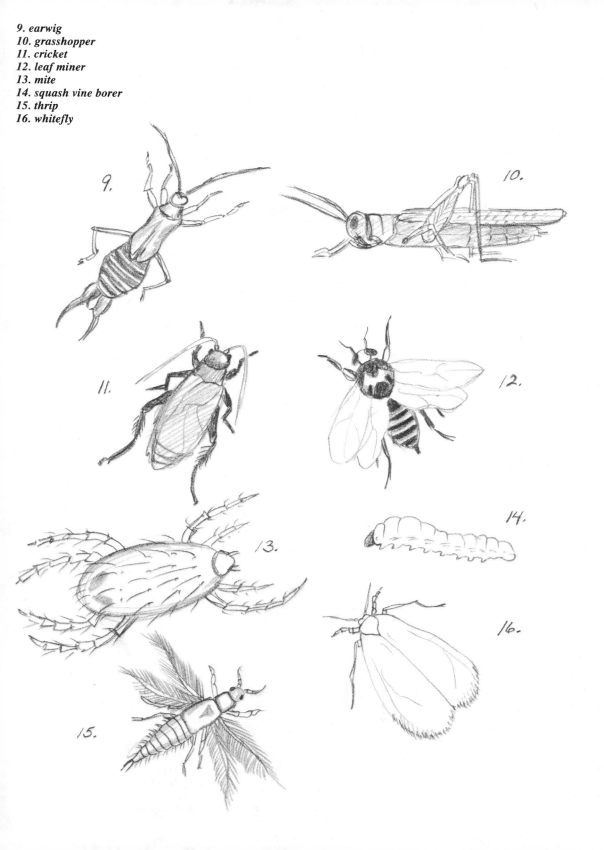

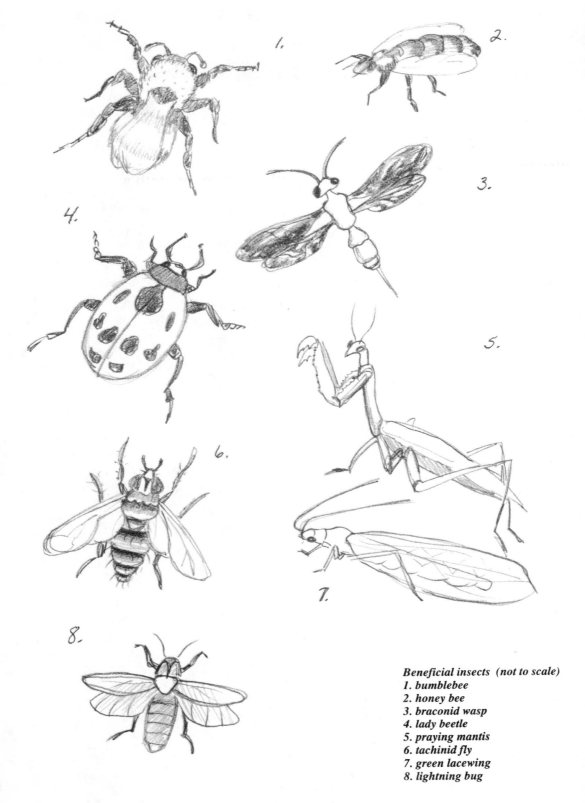

Beneficial insects (not to scale)
1. bumblebee
2. honey bee
3. braconid wasp
4. lady beetle
5. praying mantis
6. tachinid fly
7. green lacewing
8. lightning bug

Chapter Four:
From Seed To Seedling To Garden Bed

Peppers, tomatoes, eggplant, cabbage, broccoli, sprouts, and cauliflower are most often transplanted as seedlings rather than sown directly into the garden bed.

Gardeners can buy transplants from the nursery or, with a minimum amount of effort, raise the seedlings themselves.

Starting plants from seed affords the gardener selection from a wider range of varieties and increases the gardener's flexibility in respect to planting times. Another less quantifiable benefit of starting from seed is the sense of pride and accomplishment derived by witnessing and participating in the entire life cycle from seed to harvest and back to seed again.

The major factors determining seedling success are light, temperature, planting medium, and the seeds themselves.

Light

Lack of sufficient light causes the demise of many a young seedling. Long-stemmed, spindly seedlings which reach toward the light source have little chance of survival. Sunlight is the best source, but fluorescent light can be effective. The fluorescent light should be kept within three to four inches of the tops of the seedlings. General Electric's Gro and Sho is a good light source with Sylvania's Gro Lux and Westinghouse's Agro Lite both designed especially for plant use.

If you're using artificial light, remember that plants also need six to eight hours of dark time each day.

Temperature

Most seeds require a temperature between 65 and 75 degrees Fahrenheit for germination. Seedlings prosper with a temperature range of 50 to 65 degrees.

Planting Medium

Plants demand less nutrients as germinating seeds and seedlings than when they are mature. Use a disease-free soil mix which provides support and allows drainage but does not dry out or inhibit growth. You can purchase a commercial mix or make up your own by combining equal parts of garden soil, sphagnum moss and sand. Perlite and vermiculite are also good light components for a soil mix.

Pasteurize the soil by placing it in a broiler bag in the oven at 160 degrees for one-half hour. This will kill insect eggs and larvae, nematodes, viruses and many other disease organisms. This can be a rather smelly, messy process, so for small quantities, store-bought mixes are recommended.

Containers

Look for clean containers which are at least three inches deep and have good drainage capacity. Convenient styrofoam "speedling trays" with two inch individual compartments are a good choice. You can use wooden flats, clay pots, plastic flats or pots, peat pots, aluminum loaf pans, cut-down milk cartons or anything else that won't dry out too quickly.

Seeds

For standard crops, several brands of seed are available from local nurseries. Burpee, Ferry-Morse, and Northrup King are popular brands. Check expiration dates printed on the back of the seed package before purchasing.

Most seeds remain viable for at least three years, but corn, okra, pepper, and leek seeds are good for only two years; onion, parsley, and parsnip for only one. Extra seed should be stored in a cool, dry place.

For a larger variety of seeds and for more unusual kinds of vegetables, go to the seed catalogs. A list of catalogs for the home vegetable gardener can be found in Chapter One.

Here's how to start from seed:

- Begin six to eight weeks before recommended planting time, using a warm, well lighted spot.
- Presoak the seeds in warm water overnight before planting.
- Sow the seeds one-half inch apart in flats, or one in each compartment of seedling trays.
- Label each container with names of plants and dates planted. If you are starting a wide variety of seeds, assign them each a number, list them on a sheet of paper with the vegetable name, variety, date planted, source of seeds, days to maturity, and any other information you think will be useful later on. Then all you have to put on the plant label is the number assigned to that variety.
- Water only enough to keep the soil moist.
- Cover the container with a clear plastic sheet until the seeds sprout.
- Thin or transplant the seedlings after two sets of leaves have grown.
- Toughen the seedlings by withholding water and setting them outdoors gradually ten days prior to transplanting.
- Water the seedlings deeply one hour before transplanting.
- Handle the stems gently. Run a knife through the roots of any rootbound plants before transplanting.
- Dig a hole in the garden bed twice the size of the plant's soil ball, then set in the plant, fill in the hole with soil, and firm the soil around the plant.
- Protect the transplant from heat or cold and especially from drying out. Daily sprinklings and the use of shade cloth for summer plantings (or a plastic cover for rainy season plantings) may be necessary for the first two weeks.

Chapter Five:
Container Gardening

Container gardening can be viewed as an extension of raising your own seedlings. The main difference is that the gardener never transplants the seedlings into the garden, but grows them completely in containers. If you have run out of garden space in the yard and still have a few things you just *must* grow, or if you live in an apartment with no ground space at all, container gardening may be for you.

Unlike growing vegetables in the garden bed, container gardening presents the challenge of providing daily care and attention, but is generally less demanding physically than backyard gardening. Since you have a limited amount of space and soil to work with, naturally, there's less work. Also, depending upon their size, containers are usually propped up on window sills, hung from the rafters, or somehow raised from ground level, demanding less back bending from the gardener. Mobility of planters to sunnier or shadier spots in the yard is another advantage. Finally, besides providing fresh vegetables, container grown plants can be attractive additions to the home.

The six major considerations of container gardening are monitoring the sunlight, selecting the container, preparing the soil, applying fertilizers, providing water, and choosing the best varieties to plant.

Sunlight

During most of the year, California container gardeners take advantage of warm weather and sunshine, locating their containers outdoors. As long as the plants receive at least six hours of full sun, they should do well. During the heat of the summer, if the containers are movable, a spot with light shade will keep the plants from burning up and prevent the soil from drying out too quickly.

Containers

They come in all shapes, sizes and descriptions. Redwood planter boxes, clay pots, plastic tubs, wine barrels, bushel baskets, paper pulp pots, garbage cans, pails, milk cartons, coffee cans, and even plastic bags can be called into service as garden receptacles, depending on what and how much the gardener wants to raise. When using recycled containers, scrub them out well and rinse plastic or clay pots in a solution of nine parts water to one part bleach before using.

In order to produce a reasonable amount of vegetables, a container should be at least nine inches deep and hold one cubic foot of soil.

Good drainage is essential for any kind of a container, to avoid root rot. Four or more holes, 1/2 to 3/4 inches in diameter, preferably on the sides near the bottom of the container will provide adequate drainage. The drainage holes can be covered with wire meshing to keep the soil from clogging the drain.

If the container will be set upon the ground or patio deck, use cleats to lift it up slightly, permitting free water runoff, increasing air circulation, and discouraging slugs and snails.

For hanging baskets or ledge-dwelling window boxes, provide enough support, noting that one cubic foot of soil weighs from 50 to 90 pounds.

Home made garden boxes of redwood or cedar can endure the constant watering and drying out process of container gardening. Other less expensive wood can be used, but first treat it with linseed oil or copper napthenate to help it resist rotting.

Soil

The easiest way to go is to buy a bag of sterilized potting mix or a "soil-less" medium. Since container plants have such a small reservoir of soil from which to draw, it is important to have a high quality medium, rich with plant food and able to both absorb moisture and drain readily.

Garden soil can be used for transplants, but for direct seeding, sterilized soil will help prevent "damping off." This soil borne fungus causes young seedlings to collapse and die before the gardener knows what hit them. Sterilized soil, clean containers, hands, and labels are the only guards against damping off.

Dampen the soil mix well before filling the container, and leave one inch of breathing space for easier watering.

Fertilizing

Depending upon the soil mix chosen and the crops to be grown, a liquid fertilizer should be applied every one to three weeks. An alternative is to supplement the soil with a slow-release fertilizer such as Osmocote at planting time.

Peter's Professional Soluble Plant Food is a good, inexpensive commercial fertilizer. Schultz-Instant liquid plant food is another convenient product. For organic gardeners, a liquid fish emulsion, a kelp liquid, or blood and bone meal can be used.

Watering

The most vital task of container gardening is making sure the plant's roots obtain the amount of water, and then the amount of air they need. A plant can die as easily from drowning in its own pot as from drying out.

Containers dry out quickly. As soon as the top inch of soil dries out, it's time to water. This is usually a daily job during the summer, but may need to be done two to three times a day in California's hotter spots.

While checking for moisture, remove weeds and check also for signs of insects or diseases. Early detection can prevent major problems in the future.

The best time to water is early in the morning. Apply a slow, even spray of water until it seeps through the container's drainage holes.

If the gardener is 'serious' about growing vegetables in containers, a drip irrigation system such as Misti Maid or Rain Drip Vegetable garden kit will make it a lot easier. These simple systems cost less than $20 for a faucet connector, a main tube, smaller connecting tubes, and the hose end drippers.

Varieties

Recently, many vegetable varieties have been developed and highlighted especially for container growing. Some catalogs which specialize in container crops, dwarf, midget or mini varieties are: W. Atlee Burpee, Comstock, Gurney Seed & Nursery, Park Seed, and Johnny's Selected Seeds. Addresses can be found in Chapter One.

In larger containers, attractive mixes of vegetables, herbs and flowers can express the gardener's artistic nature. Flowers which are compatible with container vegetables are snapdragons, primroses, marigolds, nasturtium, petunias, zinnias, asters, and lobelia.

Basil, chives, dill, parsley, marjoram, summer savory, thyme, mint, anise and coriander are good container herbs.

Strawberries are perfectly suited for container growing. They can be cultivated in specially designed "strawberry pots" or in any container at least nine inches deep, with plants six inches apart.

Crop	Plant Size	Container Size (minimum)	Cultural Notes
Beans	1-2 feet	8-10 in. deep 10 gallon pot	harvest beans while young and tender
Beets	10-12 in.	10-12 in. deep 3-7 gallon	eat leaves & roots, plant 2-3 in. apart
Broccoli	12-18 in.	1 plant:3-5 gal. 3 plants: 7 gal.	quick crop, start from transplant
Brussels Sprouts	12-18 in.	same as broccoli	feed and water frequently
Carrots	10-12 in.	10-12 in. deep 7 gal. for 10-15 carrots	use light, loose soil
Cauliflower	10-12 in.	same as broccoli	same as broccoli
Cucumbers	3-5 ft.	1 plant:1 gal. 3-4 plants: 3-4 gal.	support vines with trellises
Eggplant	1-3 ft.	1 plant: 3 gal. 3 plants: 10 gal.	start from transplant
Lettuce	6-10 in.	6-8 plants:3-5 gal.	interplant with other crops
Melons	3-5 ft.	2 vines: 10 gal.	select short vine varieties
Onions	10-12 in.	8-10 in. deep	start from sets, harvest as green onions
Peppers	2-3 ft.	1 plant: 3 gal. 2 plants:5 gal.	start from transplants
Radishes	6-8 in.	plant with others	versatile, fast
Squash	2-3 ft.	3-4 plants: 5 gal.	keep fruit picked
Tomatoes	2-5 ft.	1 dwarf: 3 gal. 1 cherry: 5 gal. 1 standard: 10-20gal.	stake mature plant, start from transplant

Part Two— The Vegetables

This section contains everything the gardener would ever want to know about the most popular garden vegetables.

For each vegetable chapter, these subjects are discussed:

- Vital Statistics — basic cultural information,
- Roots and Rumors — a history of the plant, and
- How-to—detailed planting through harvesting information, including problems and solutions.

A plant climate zone is an area in which a set of similar environmental conditions determines a set of similar garden planting and harvesting practices. Some of the factors determining an area's plant climate zone are its temperature ranges, distance from the equator, elevation, distance from the coast, position in relation to mountains and hills, and local terrain.

Most gardening books include a map of the United States with the different zones drawn out to help the gardener determine when to plant. Because of California's amazing climatic diversity, almost every zone in America runs through California. In Sunset's *New Western Garden Book*, California boasts 21 out of the 24 plant climate zones of the western states.

The Seed-to-Harvest Calender in Appendix A is tailored to California's inland valleys and hills as shown in green on the map on the back cover. Mountain gardeners can plant their crops in May and June. Coastal and desert dwellers can check with the University of California Cooperative Extension Office for the best planting times. They are listed in Appendix D.

Appendix C provides information abut the monthly normal temperatures for California cities. This information will help you determine if seeds will germinate and how long it will take in your particular area. In the Vital Statistics section for each vegetable, the preferred soil temperature for germination is listed. While soil temperature and air temperature varies slightly, these normal air temperatures are pretty good indicators, if you don't want to invest in a soil thermometer.

Average and record frost dates can be found in Appendix B. The more adventurous the gardener, the closer the plantings are to the average frost date. Part of the fun of gardening is challenging the weather and harvesting the first crop of the season, or the latest in the fall. The practical yet ambitious gardener may choose to start a few plants well before the recommended planting dates, and the rest on the regular schedule.

44

Cabbages
Vital Statistics

Common name: The Cabbage or 'Cole' Crops
- heading plants: broccoli, Brussels sprouts, cabbage, cauliflower
- leafy greens: collard, kale, mustard
- root crops: kohlrabi, radish, rutabaga, turnip

Botanical name: Brassica, spp.

Family: Cruciferae - Latin for "cross-bearing" (Mustard)

Season: cool season crops

Site: Full sun or partial shade (6-8 hours sun each day)

Plants per person:
6-8 broccoli	12-16 kohlrabi
4-5 Brussels sprouts	12-16 rutabaga
4-6 cabbage, cauliflower	25-30 turnips
10-15 greens	40-50 radishes

Soil requirements: pH 6.0-6.8, sandy loam soil or raised beds for clay soils, well fortified with organic matter

Seed germination: 3-7 days at 75 degrees F. soil temperature

Plant size: broccoli and Brussels sprouts: 2-4 feet tall
cabbage: 1-3 feet spread
cauliflower: 2 feet tall
chinese cabbage: 18-20 inches
greens and root crops: 6-18 inches

Days to maturity: broccoli: 50-80 days
Brussels sprouts: 90 days
cabbage: 50-100 days
cauliflower: 55-70 days
greens and root crops: 7-50 days

Plant with: aromatic plants, beets onions, leaf lettuce

Avoid planting with: strawberries, tomatoes, pole beans

Roots and Rumors

The elders of the mustard family are the green leafy vegetables, with the most ancient, mustard greens, originating in northwest India before written history.

The kissing cousins of the cole family, collards and kale, sprung up in the eastern Mediterranean area and Asia Minor. These primitive coles have persisted as a food source for over 4000 years. Kale is sometimes referred to as the curly collard, or even more distinctively as "cabbage waves" by the Spanish. In Pharoah Akhenton's tomb, the sarcophagus was lined with kale leaves carved of jade so they would never shrivel. Inhabitants of the British Isles have attributed mystical powers to the kale.

Cabbage is another senior member of the mustard family. It originated from a wild, loose-headed variety also of Asia Minor and the eastern Mediterranean region, along with broccoli and cauliflower. A food staple in Europe and North Africa for thousands of years, cabbage inspired ancient Egyptians to raise altars in its honor and starred in Greek fables as "a gift from the father of the gods." Radishes were also highly regarded by the Greeks who cast replicas of them in gold.

Broccoli was the favorite cole crop of the Romans, and is still favored by Italians today. Caesar and his contemporaries loved broccoli so passionately that it was served twice and even three times during a single meal, usually prepared the same way. Broccoli was boiled then "bruised" with a mixture of cumin, coriander seeds, chopped onions plus a few drops of oil and "sun made" wine, according to the Roman writer, Apicus.

It seems that Drussus, the eldest son of Emperor Tiberius, was so addicted to this recipe that he ate nothing but broccoli for a month. He gave up broccoli only when his urine turned bright green and his father scolded him for 'living precariously.'

When the Romans brought broccoli to England it was

dubbed "Italian asparagus" or "sprout cauliflower." Broccoli came to California in the 1920's. In Europe, cauliflower is known as "cavoli a fiore" (the cabbage that blooms like a flower). Mark Twain claimed that cauliflower "is just a cabbage with a college education."

The kindergarteners of the mustard family are the Brussels sprouts, kohlrabi, turnips and rutabaga. Turnips are believed to have originated in Siberia and the yellow rutabagas or "Swede turnips" so popular on the European continent probably evolved there from the turnip.

Another turnip descendant, the kohlrabi, was rumored to have been introduced to western Europe from Asia by Atilla the Hun. The word kohlrabi is of Teutonic origin, translating literally to "a cabbage turnip."

Records of cultivation go back only 500 years for the kohlrabi and Brussels sprouts. Believing they enhanced the diner's mental agility, the Romans highly prized the then rare Brussels sprouts. Somehow, they were introduced to Brussels where they flourished, picked up their present name, and became a source of Flemish national pride.

How-to

Keep the coles cool. By planting them early enough in the spring, or preferably in late summer or early fall, they will mature prior to extreme summer heat. A generous application of mulch around the heading coles, six to eight inches deep, early in the summer will keep the soil temperature down and will also provide extra nutrients.

The cabbage greens and root crops are light feeders and prosper in most soils. Cabbages are not as particular as broccoli, Brussels sprouts or cauliflower, but they are all heavy feeders requiring high levels of nitrogen, phosphorus and potassium.

One week or more before planting, the gardener can work one to one-and-a-half pounds of steer manure per square foot of garden area into the top six inches of soil. For an extra boost, one side-dressing of dehydrated manure or a commercial fertilizer during the growing season is advised for all heading cole crops, except cabbages, which experience splitting heads from too much fertilizer or water.

Cauliflowers are most sensitive to the heat and also to salty soil, acidic soil, or drought. All of the cole crops require deep, even, and regular irrigation to compensate for weak root systems.

The cole greens will tolerate a wider range of environmental conditions. Kohlrabi, that odd, bulging green globe, is also impervious to temperature variations and boasts immunity from the insects and diseases common to the other cole crops.

The cole greens and root crops do well with a direct seeding into the garden bed. Broccoli, Brussels sprouts, cabbage and cauliflowers are most often started from seeds indoors or transplanted from nursery grown seedlings.

To start seedlings indoors, plant seeds in potting soil one-half inch apart and one-quarter to one-half inch deep. Moisten the soil, cover with plastic and keep warm. When the seedlings appear, remove the plastic, water once or twice a week and apply a small dose of liquid fertilizer once a week.

Harden off seedlings by setting them outside for a few hours each day, gradually increasing their outdoor stay for seven to ten days, at which time they can be transplanted.

Water the seedlings well before setting them into moistened holes, four to eight inches deep. A small handful of compost or 5-10-10 fertilizer may be dropped into the bottom of each hole and covered with one to two inches of soil before planting. Secure the cutworm collar around the stem and fill the hole with soil. Make sure that the plants are no deeper than the level of the first set of leaf stems. Press the soil gently around the plant and water again.

Problems and Solutions

The cabbage looper, cabbage worm, cutworm, snails and slugs, the harlequin bug and aphids are the major cole pests. Attack and Dipel are biological insecticides which are very effective against the cabbage looper and the cabbage worm.

"Cutworm collars" can protect plants from the gnawing nuisance of that pest. A two to three inch strip of newspaper or cardboard, or a tuna can with both ends removed make good collars. Place the collars one to two inches above and below the soil. These protective devices can remain in place all season.

Harlequin bugs have bright red markings on their black shield-shaped bodies. They are easily spotted and can be handpicked from the plants if discovered before too many appear.

Aphids are extremely troublesome to the heading cole crops, especially broccoli and Brussels sprouts. They can be found on the undersides of leaves, and eventually within the flower buds. A fall planting of these crops can move up harvest time to a point where they mature before the aphids become active, depending upon the weather. Aphids start flying and settling upon the cole crops between the end of March and the beginning of May, and then again from mid-September to late October. Once these pests are spotted on the plants, the gardener can try spraying them away with the garden hose. Malathion is the chemical control most often used against aphids.

Fungus diseases are sometimes a troublesome condition of cole crops. Through crop rotation, well-drained soil and selections of resistant varieties, most insect and disease problems of cole crops can be avoided.

Peppers
Vital Statistics

Common name:	PEPPERS
Botanical name:	Capsicum anuum
Family:	Solanaceae (Nightshade)
Season:	warm season crop
Site:	full sun
Plants per person:	three to four sweet peppers, two hot
Soil requirements:	pH 5.5-7.0, sandy or loamy soil, well fortified with organic matter
Seed germination:	eight days at 77-86 degrees F. soil temperature
Plant size:	bushy plant, 14-48 inches high, depending upon variety
Days to maturity:	65-80 days (from transplanting to mature green stage)
Plant with:	onions, parsley, asparagus
Avoid planting with:	cabbages, potatoes

Roots and Rumors

Christopher Columbus may have been a top-rate navigator, but he wasn't much of a botanist. In his effort to seek a shorter route to the spices of the Indies, he stumbled upon a new continent and a new condiment. Instead of Piper nigrum, the black pepper berries so prized by the Europeans, Columbus' crew stocked the hold of one entire ship with the native American plant, Capsicum annuum.

The new plant was well received in the homeland and proudly named "Spanish pepper." After Columbus first discovered the attractive red and green peppers on his first voyage in 1492, other explorers to the New World encountered many forms of peppers in the tropical areas of Central and South America.

Pepper-like fruits were embroidered upon Indian garments and depicted in pottery unearthed near the coast of Peru, dating back to about the first century. Artifacts found in ancient ruins of the Olmecs, Torecs, and Aztecs indicate cultivation of peppers and extensive use of them in their diets.

How-to

Two elements essential for pepper propagation are warmth and Magnesium. Peppers are usually started from transplants, primarily because of their aversion to cold weather and soil. If the plants are set out before the temperature reaches 55 degrees F., the waxy leaves curl up in protest and the pepper refuses to produce until warmer weather prevails.

A fortification of the soil with well rotted manure or a balanced commercial fertilizer (5-10-10) at planting time and a side-dressing of the same at blossom time should supply all the Magnesium and other nutrients the peppers need.

Starting seedlings indoors allows the gardener a wider selection of varieties than is available at the nurseries. In a seedling tray filled with sterilized potting mix, sow seeds one half inch deep, two inches apart, and cover lightly with vermiculite or sphagnum moss. Transplant into three inch pots once the plants reach three to four inches, fertilizing once a week.

Hardening off the plants by exposing them to the outside world little by little over a ten day period will help reduce the shock of transplant.

Using raised beds allows for earlier planting, since they usually heat up faster than flat garden beds. They also encourage deep root growth necessary for maximum pepper production.

All varieties of peppers turn red when they are ripe, even the yellow and golden ones. Peppers can be harvested when they are green or ripe. Picking peppers while they are still green hastens future fruit set. Fresh peppers can be stored in the refrigerator for up to two weeks.

If the gardener is growing chili peppers for drying, wait until they turn red before harvesting, and then hang them in a sunny place until they are dry and brittle.

Hot peppers and most sweet peppers contain a substance called capsaicin which causes the hotness. Capasicin is found in tiny sacs between the lining and the inner wall of the pepper.

A hot pepper planted next to a sweet pepper will not transmit its heat to its neighbor. Even so, it's a good idea to separate the sweet and hot peppers in the garden, if only to avoid mixups. Anyone who has mistakenly taken a big bite out of a hot pepper will readily support this suggestion.

When working with extra hot varieties, gardeners are advised to wear rubber gloves to protect against skin burns.

Abel Chacon, a California pepper aficionado, says, "If you want 'em really hot, don't water the plants for seven to ten days, then pick them in the morning while they are crisp and fresh."

Almost any pepper variety can be grown in a container. One plant can be grown in a three gallon container, or two in a five gallon tub. Peppers can spend the whole growing season in a pot, or they can spend the summer in the garden bed, then be potted up and brought indoors when the weather cools down.

For a mature garden-grown plant, find a 10-14 inch diameter pot. Soak the plant for two hours before digging. Dig straight down around the plant's drip line, then gently lift the plant out of the ground and place it in the pot. Fill the pot with soil, soak it well, then bring it into a sunny spot indoors. When new blossoms appear, transfer the pollen from one flower to another with a cotton swab.

Peppers come in all shapes, sizes, and colors. The tiny Tabasco and Thai hot peppers pack a red hot wave far greater than their size might suggest. Red Cayenne, Serrano, Jalapeno and Anaheim M are long, tapered, hot chili pepper varieties. Similar in appearance to the chili pepppers, but sweet and mild to the taste, Hungarian Sweet Wax, Sweet Banana and Burpee's Early Pimento are especially good for pickling.

Problems and Solutions

When planting peppers in the garden bed, a plastic milk carton with both ends cut off serves as a good cutworm collar and protects young seedlings from spring winds.

Spacing of the plants depends upon the varieties, but should be arranged so that the leaves of adjacent plants will touch when full grown (usually 12-14 inches apart.) By placing the plants close together, their leafy canopy will shade out weeds, help maintain a steady soil temperature, and protect the fruit from sunburn.

A mulch can be applied in the summer to retain moisture. Deep, regular watering will help prevent blossom end rot which appears as a big black sunken ring on the base of the pepper.

Although peppers are subject to the same insects and diseases as their cousins the tomatoes, they seldom succumb to such conditions. Refer to the tomato section for detailed information and solutions.

Tomatoes

Vital Statistics

Common name:	TOMATO
Botanical name:	Lycopersicon lycopersicum
Family:	Solanaceae (Nightshade, along with peppers, eggplant and potatoes)
Season:	warm season crop
Site:	full sun or partial shade
Plants per person:	one to four plants, depending upon appetite, canning, and freezing capacity
Soil requirements::	pH 6.2-6.8, slightly acidic; sandy to sandy-loams for early varieties, heavier soils for main crop and late varieties.
Seed germination:	six days at 77-86 degrees F. soil temperature eight days at 68 degrees 43 days at 50 degrees
Plant size:	two to eight feet tall, rambling or bush-like, depending upon variety
Days to maturity:	50-80
Plant with:	onions, parsley, chives, basil, asparagus, carrots, nasturtium
Avoid planting with:	cabbages, potatoes

Roots and Rumors

"These apples, as also the whole plant, chill the body... wherefore it is dangerous to make use of them. They give little nourishment to the body and that little is bad and corrupt."

So wrote French botanist Dalechamps in 1653 about the tomato, the same fruit that was so cherished by the ancient Maya, Inca and Aztec civilizations. Probably originating in the Andean region of South America, the tomato slowly moved northward to Mexico where the Aztecs considered it a symbol of good fortune from the gods. In fact, 'tomatl' is the Aztecan word from which 'tomato' is derived.

In spite of its long history and wide use in the Americas, this New World plant met with hysterical reactions upon its debut in Europe. Introduced to Spain in 1525, the tomato was at first considered a curiosity, then poisonous (the leaves and stems of the plant *are* toxic), and finally as a sinful aphrodisiac.

Matthiolus, the first European botanist to examine the tomato called it "mala insana," unwholesome fruit. By the seventeenth century, the tomato's common name had become "pomo d'amour," or love apple.

When British botanist Miller was given the task of classifying it, he assigned the name: "Lycopersicon," (Latin for wolf-peach). This official botanical name is still used today.

Indeed, the early European botanists had a field day with the tomato. Even with such adamant condemnations, by as early as 1560, growing numbers of courageous, or perhaps sensuous, Italians grew tomatoes in their gardens.

They were reintroduced to America in the eighteenth century, with the first daring cultivation noted in Thomas Jefferson's garden in 1781. Not until the early twentieth century did fresh consumption of the tomato become popular. Today, at least half of the people in the United States grow their own for that special flavor and texture attributed exclusively to home-grown tomatoes.

How-to

Join the legions of lycopersicon lovers and grow your own tomatoes. In the valleys, they grow like weeds, requiring very little effort on the gardener's part. Local nurseries offer a plentiful choice of varieties. It is almost as easy, though, to start your own plants from seeds between the end of January and mid-March.

Tomatoes are not quite as sensitive to the cold as peppers, but they should be set outdoors gradually during the day for ten days prior to transplanting. Withhold water for several days before transplanting, then water deeply immediately before settling them into the garden bed.

Roots can dive to a depth of four to five feet into the soil. The plants thrive in a deep soil rich with organic matter. Before planting, add a good helping of dehydrated manure, compost or a commercial fertilizer to the bottom of the hole and cover with two to three inches of soil. No further fertilization should be necessary.

Tomato plants like to be buried deeply into the soil. By covering a good deal of the stem, the above-ground portion will grow thick and strong while the underground part will grow roots to better anchor the plant and draw nutrients and water from the soil. The use of a post-hole digger to scoop a deep, loose soil column for the plant is quite effective.

Once the seedlings are cozily entrenched in the garden bed, water deeply and continue to irrigate deeply every seven to ten days thereafter. A four to six inch mulch around the plants, when the soil is well warmed late in the spring, will help retain moisture and reduce weed growth.

Almost all varieties, even the new bush-like ones, need support to keep the vines and fruit up off the ground. Gardeners show great ingenuity in devising support systems, from scrap-heap specials to elaborate tomato towers. The elementary individual staking method meets the needs of most small scale gardeners. Six to eight foot stakes driven one foot deep into the soil, spaced three to five inches from the plant at transplanting time will support the plant throughout the growing season. As the plant begins to lean, tie the stem loosely to the stake with a cloth strip or other soft material.

Tomato cages are even easier to use than stakes, but slightly more expensive. They should be at least five feet tall, 24 inches in diameter, and fastened to the ground with two short stakes to avoid toppling.

If the gardener is an apartment dweller or has limited space, growing tomatoes in containers can be quite successful. Dwarf, bush or compact varieties will produce in containers with as little as two or three gallons of soil. Most seed companies now offer tomatoes especially suited for container cultivation. Most of the full-sized varieties need 10 to 20 gallon containers.

The latest development in container gardening is the use of a bag of commercial potting soil as both the plant's soil medium and its container. The soil company advises planting one tomato in a 16 quart bag or two to three tomatoes in a 32 quart bag.

Dozens of tomato varieties are available to the home gardener. It's a good idea to plant an assortment: an early tomato, one main crop variety, cherry tomatoes and an Italian or plum tomato for freezing. Freezing Italian tomatoes is the easiest way to preserve them. Place ripe, clean fruit on a cookie sheet in the freezer. Once they become hard as rocks, toss them into a plastic bag and store in the freezer until cooking time. Frozen tomatoes can be taken from the bag and added directly to the spaghetti sauce, soup kettle, or other tomato-based dish.

Problems and Solutions

To avoid insect and disease problems, try to follow these cultural practices:

- grow Verticilium and Fusarium Wilt resistant varieties (VF on the plant label)

- select healthy plants with thick stems, dark green leaves and no blossoms (check under the leaves for insects)
- rotate crops
- handle plants only when necessary
- allow intervals of one week or more between watering, if possible
- don't smoke near plants to prevent tobacco mosaic virus
- remove severely diseased plants from the garden
- do not prune or pinch back vines (can cause sunburned tomatoes)

Blossom-end rot, that unsightly leathery scar on the bottom of the tomato, often happens when the plant experiences a sudden hot, dry spell. Special attention to irrigation when the temperatures exceed 90 degrees F. and a moisture-retaining mulch can help prevent this malady. Rotating crops and growing tomatoes in a well drained soil will help prevent anthracnose and leaf spot.

Another common problem of tomato growers is fruit set failure. Cold spring nights when the temperature dips below 55 degrees F. or consistently hot summer days, when temperatures exceed 90 degrees F. often hamper fruit set. Following the proper planting schedule lessens the chances of temperature-related fruit set failure. Low light intensity or high ozone levels (smog) can also affect fruit set.

Pests include snails, slugs, cutworms, tomato fruit worms, tomato hornworms, stink bugs, leafhoppers, aphids, flea beetles, white flies, and nematodes. Selecting varieties that are nematode resistant is the best deterrent to the root knot nematode. Cutworm collars can protect plants against that pest; hand picking is recommended for snails, slugs, hornworms and stink bugs. Some people have found the task of pulling those bright green hornworms from the plants so distasteful that they have trained their trusty canines to search out and swallow the nasty creatures. Many dogs actually enjoy the taste of the hornworms. Dipel and Attack are biological insecticides that can be used against the hornworms, fruit worms, and other caterpillars.

Stink bugs come in larger numbers than hornworms and can cause great damage. These green to brownish gray, shield-shaped insects cause light-colored cloudy spots with corky areas in the tissue of the fruit just below the skin. No chemical control is registered for use against the stink bug, so hand picking is the only viable alternative.

Soapy water sprays, yellow sticky traps, and pyrethrum are the nonchemical controls for aphids and white flies. Malathion can also be used against these two insects, as well as flea beetles. To discourage flea beetles and leafhoppers, a thick layer of mulch can be applied.

EGGPLANT

Vital Statistics

Common name:	EGGPLANT
Botanical name:	Solanum melongena
Family:	Solanaceae (Nightshade)
Season:	warm season crop
Site:	full sun
Plants per person:	two to three
Soil requirements:	pH 5.5-7.2, slightly heavy soil, well fortified with organic matter, high Phosporus content
Seed germination:	eight days at 77 degrees F. soil temperature 10-15 days at 68-86 degrees F.
Plant size:	two to four feet tall
Days to maturity:	55-85
Plant with:	beans, peppers
Avoid planting with:	corn

Roots and Rumors

Like all other members of the Nightshade family, the eggplant has been associated with insanity and evil because of its poisonous cousin, Belladonna. The ancient Arabic word for eggplant which survives yet today means "senseless fool."

Eggplant probably originated in India, spread eastward to China by the fifth century, B.C., then later travelled the trade routes to Spain and Africa.

English herbalist John Gerard in 1597 described the eggplant as being "of the bignesse of a Swan's egge... of a white colour, sometimes yellow, and often browne." The deep purple varieties most common today were not cultivated in Gerard's days. The light colored and multi-colored eggplants of the past are now making a strong comeback, along with increased cultivation of the thin Oriental varieties.

How-to

The subtle beauty of the small lavender flowers of the eggplant provide a delicate accent to the plants' velvety gray-green leaves. Their beauty alone almost makes it worthwhile to plant these bushy wonders.

Eggplant culture is very similar to tomatoes. They are easy to start from seed, or can be found as seedlings in most nurseries in the spring.

To transplant, dig a hole twice the size of the container, add a layer of compost or a handful of a commercial fertilizer (10-10-10), cover with two inches of soil, set the plant into the hole and fill it with soil. Water deeply once or twice a week. Unlike tomatoes, eggplants stand erect and require no support.

Harvest eggplants while the skin is shiny purple and when they have reached the desired size (the smaller the better). They can be stored in the refrigerator for up to ten days.

Problems and Solutions

Eggplants are susceptible to the same insects and diseases

as tomatoes, but to a much lesser extent. See the tomato section for remedies.

Potatoes
Vital Statistics

Common name:	POTATO
Botanical name:	Solanum tuberosum
Family:	Solanaceae (Nightshade Family)
Season:	cool weather crop
Site:	full sun
Plants per person:	20-30
Soil requirements:	pH 5.0-6.5, slightly acidic; sandy loam is best, loose texture, well drained
Seed germination:	potato "shoots" appear in two to three weeks
Plant size:	above ground vines grow to three feet high
Days to maturity:	13-17 weeks
Plant with:	beans, corn, cabbage, eggplant
Avoid planting with:	squash, tomatoes

Roots and Rumors

Peruvians planted potatoes as long as 4,000 years ago. When Spanish explorer Pizarro discovered these "earth nuts" in Peru, he sent a sample back to Europe in 1537.

After conducting thorough scientific experiments, the Royal Society of London proclaimed that the potato was a nutritious food for the poor. Following this proclamation, in 1586, Sir Walter Raleigh sent a shipment of potatoes to his estate in Ireland. They became extremely popular there, as evidenced by the fact that Irish factory workers were allotted 12 pounds of potatoes per day until early in the nineteenth century.

Unfortunately, Ireland's dependence upon a few varieties of potato led to the death of more than one million people when a fungus (Phytophthora infestans) wiped out entire potato harvests in the 1840's.

Sympathetic officials of the Commonwealth of Massachusetts offered a $10,000 reward for "a sure and practical remedy for the Potato Rot." The singular saviour was a wild potato from Chile which was discovered to be resistant to the blight. Today a wide diversity of potato varieties is cultivated, regionally adapted to different climates around the world.

How-to

"Pray for peace and grace and spiritual food,
For wisdom and guidance, for all these are good,
But don't forget the potato."

Prayer and Potatoes
John Tyler Pette, 1822-1907

In the garden, as in prayer, the potato is often forgotten at planting time. Their lush green vines, very similar to their cousins the tomatoes, are a welcomed addition to any garden. The sweet, fresh spuds are a diner's delight, hardly resembling their store-bought counterparts.

The potato itself is not a root or a fruit, but a bulging portion of the plant's underground stem. The tricky part of growing potatoes is to plant them as soon as the threat of frost has passed, but soon enough that harvest time occurs before the heat sets in. Tuberization (the formation of the potato) decreases slightly as the temperature exceeds 68 degrees F. and stops almost completely in temperatures above 84 degrees F.

Fall potatoes benefit from July heat with lush vegetative growth. As the weather cools, tubers begin to form. With any luck, the gardener can harvest potatoes for Thanksgiving, prior to the first frost. This plant is extremely sensitive to frost.

Potatoes need a steady supply of water throughout their growing period. They do not compete well with weeds, so either apply a thick mulch or pull weeds regularly to maintain a prolific patch.

Ruth Stout's method for planting potatoes was to form a mound of mulch, toss in the seed pieces, rearrange the mulch to cover the potatoes, and let them grow. In hot, dry climates, this method is not quite as successful, but growing them in a raised bed, fortified with organic matter will meet their needs.

Simply dig a four to six inch trench in the middle of the bed and place a handful of compost or a small amount of commercial fertilizer (10-10-10) every ten to 12 inches along the trench. Situate the seed potatoes between each compost mound and cover with three to four inches of soil.

To avoid "greening" of potatoes, "hill" them a couple of times during the season. This is accomplished by pulling up the soil around the stems, thus keeping the potatoes from poking out of the soil.

It is time to dig up the potato crop when the vines have died back completely and the potato skin ceases to slip from pressure of the thumb. Use a garden fork or hoe to gently lift the potatoes from the soil. Most of the potatoes will be found in the top six inches of soil. Harvesting potatoes is a delightful task for young ones in the family, just like digging for a buried treasures.

"New" potatoes will keep in the refrigerator for three to four weeks. Mature, dry potatoes should be kept in a cool, damp, dark place at all times.

Some seed catalogs offer seed potatoes, but it is usually easier to pick them up from your local nursery. Make sure the seed is certified.

Problems and Solutions

The poisons found in potato leaves deter many insects while good cultural practices will lessen disease problems. The Colorado potato beetle and the flea beetle are two chewing insects that attack potato foliage. Handpicking the beetles from the plants or treating them with rotenone, pyrethrum, or malathion will decrease their numbers.

Leaf hoppers and aphids are sucking insects that damage potatoes. A spray of a strong stream of water from a garden hose will dislodge aphids from the plants, and muslin canopies over young potato plants for one month will discourage leaf hoppers from laying their eggs on the plant leaves.

Wireworms, white grubs, and cutworms are soil borne insects that feed on the tubers. These insects are difficult to control, and planting in the area where they have been a problem in the past should be avoided.

There are more than 60 diseases of potato plants. Verticilium wilt and scab disease are the two most common diseases in California. Crop rotation, planting certified seed, and careful handling of the seed potatoes will prevent most of the diseases. Try not to plant potatoes in the same spot without a three year break, and avoid planting potatoes where you have had tomatoes, peppers, or eggplant in the preceding year.

A Potato Substitute- The Jerusalem Artichoke

Less finicky than the potato, the Jerusalem artichoke offers an interesting alternative to the home gardener. Perhaps you have seen these odd, knobby tubers in the grocery store produce department. It is hard to imagine that the same plants which produce these homely underground spuds also sport bright yellow sunflowers on stems five to eight feet tall.

Before planting this hardy herbaceaous perennial, consider the "choke" side of its character. Not only will the plant choke out weeds, but also any other crops in its vicinity. If the gardener misses harvesting any tubers in the fall, they will greet you in the spring with fresh new sprouts. This persistence can be an asset, however, if you have a corner of the garden in which to confine the 'chokes.

These plants are not particular about their environment and are seldom bothered by insects or diseases. They prefer a sunny spot with well drained soil. Plant them in early spring or fall as you would potatoes. Set the tubers (either whole or pieces with two or three prominent buds) into the ground four to five inches deep, ten to 18 inches apart in rows three feet apart.

Water deeply but not too often. Harvest any time after the leaves turn yellow in the fall. You can store the tubers most easily by leaving them in the ground until you are ready to use them. They are not damaged by frost. On the contrary, their taste seems to improve with cold soil conditions.

Cut off the large woody tops before harvesting and carefully dig out the 'chokes to avoid cuts and bruises. Store in a dry, cool place, preferably the refrigerator. Serve as a sliced raw vegetable for salads or dips, steamed or boiled like potatoes, or in a stir fry dish in place of water chestnuts.

SQUASH

Vital Statistics

Common name:	SQUASH, CUCUMBERS, MELONS, PUMPKINS, GOURDS
Botanical name:	Cucurbita, spp.
Family:	Cucurbitaceae (the Gourd Family, along with cucumbers, melons, pumpkins, and gourds)
Season:	warm season crop
Site:	full sun
Plants per person:	two to three
Soil requirements:	pH 5.5-6.8, well drained sandy loam well fortified with compost or manure. Plant in mounds or on raised beds if soil is heavy clay.
Seed germination:	three to five days at 80 degrees F. soil temperature. Will germinate in soil temperatures from 70 to 95 degrees F.
Plant size:	rambling vines or more compact bush varieties spread from three to 12 feet
Days to maturity:	50-80
Plant with:	corn, beans, peas, radishes
Avoid planting with:	cabbages, potatoes

Roots and Rumors

The Narragansett Indians called it "askutasquash," the Iroquois "isquoutersquash," and the algonquins "askoot." For convenience sake, early European settlers shortened this vegetable's name to plain "squash."

Indigenous to the Western Hemisphere, the squash is among the oldest of cultivated plants in America. Ancient Indians called it "the apple of God" since squash seeds were believed to increase fertility. Squash was a staple food of Indian tribes all over what is now the United States, and was the first dish they taught the colonists how to cook.

Not only did the new Americans learn how to cook squash, they also devised new uses for this crop. In 1611, Elisabeth Skinner of Roanoke, Virginia wrote:

"The seeds (of certain squash) pounded with meale and their own sweet iuyces...doth beautifie the face, for it taketh away freckles and al spottes...if the place be well rubbed with it- in the sonne's light."

How-to

Whether you're growing squash for culinary or cosmetic purposes, give it plenty of space, at least eight hours of sunshine, a steady supply of water, a rich loose soil and you will receive a bumper crop beyond your wildest dreams, perhaps even beyond your most horrific nightmare.

Soil preparation is the key to squash cultivation. The plants need a loose soil at least 12 inches deep for their far- reaching tap roots. With the addition of large quantities of organic matter such as compost, manure, old leaves, grass clippings, hay, or kitchen scraps to the garden bed before planting, no further fertilization should be required for these heavy feeders. One way to provide the organic matter is to dig a furrow two feet deep where the row of squash will be planted. Bury one foot of organic matter in the bottom of the furrow, then refill the other foot of the furrow with garden soil. Squash seeds which have been soaked in warm water for 24 hours can then be planted on top of the bed with summer squash plants thinned to 10-12 inches apart, winter squash 12-18 inches apart.

Squash also grows well in hills, with five plants to a hill, spacing summer squash hills four to six feet apart and winter squash six to ten feet apart.

Another place to grow squash is on top or around the edges of an old compost pile. The plants get plenty of nourishment and the vines camouflage the sometimes unsightly heaps.

Summer squash should be harvested almost daily to prevent the creation of those monster squash, the ones that got away. All squash are best picked when they are small and slightly immature. Cutting the fruit from the plant rather than pulling or twisting it off makes for a cleaner harvest.

Summer and winter squash can be grown in containers of at least five gallon capacity. Dwarf or bush-type varieties are easiest to contain. A good arrangement is planting three bush-type squash in a ten gallon container.

Summer squash varieties mature considerably faster than the winter squashes. While summer squash is usually consumed fresh, winter varieties are often better suited for cold storage and use throughout the winter.

Squash Relatives

Cucumbers, melons, pumpkins, and gourds are all members of the Cucurbit Family. The cucurbit cousins have widely differing places of origin. Pumpkins, like squash, are native to the Americas. Cucumbers were probably from eastern Asia or Africa. Watermelons are indigenous to south central Africa and other melons probably sprang up in Africa or Persia.

In spite of their varied heritages, in general, cultural practices, insect and disease problems described for squash hold true for growing these crops as well. Here are a few cultural tips specific to the squash relatives:

Pumpkins. Never let the soil dry out completely. Leave only one pumpkin on each vine for a giant jack. Plant in hills eight to ten feet apart, four to six seeds per hill, one inch deep, thinned to two vigorous plants per hill. If you are planting in rows, allow six to ten feet between rows, with one plant every two to three feet.

Cucumbers. Harvest all mature fruit regularly to keep vines in full production. Grow on a trellis to save space. Plant in hills four to five feet apart, four to five seeds per hill, one half inch deep, thinned to two to three plants per hill. If planting in rows, allow four feet between rows, four to six inches between seeds, thinned to eight to ten inches between plants.

Melons. Withhold water a few days before harvest to heighten flavor. Grow on a strong trellis to save space. Support the fruit once it reaches fist size with "slings" made of old onion bags, plastic netting, or nylons, tied to the trellis. Plant in hills five feet apart, with three to five seeds per hill, one half inch deep, thinned to two to three plants per hill. If planting in rows, allow six feet between rows with three to four seeds in a grouping two feet apart, thinned to one plant in each grouping.

Watermelons. The fruit is ripe when its bottom spot turns from white to creamy yellow. Plant hills six to eight feet apart, with five to six seeds per hill, one half inch deep, thinned to two to three plants per hill. Row planting is the same as other melons.

Problems and Solutions

One condition for squash production over which the gardener has no control is the weather. If the weather is not to the liking of the honeybees, particularly if it is too cold for them to leave the hive, they will not venture out to pollinate. The honeybee is the primary squash pollinator, transferring pollen from the smaller male flowers to the larger female flowers on the same or neighboring plants. The female flowers open early in the morning and are receptive to pollination for only one day. If the bee misses this one shot, the flower will wilt and die.

Squash, melons, and cucumbers will not cross-pollinate, but varieties within the same species will. The only time this will cause a problem is when a gardener saves seeds from one year to the next.

Conditions which set the stage for insect and disease problems can be controlled to some degree by the gardener. Buying resistant varieties of seed will prevent Fusarium and Verticilium wilt. Choosing fresh, certified seed will lessen chances of other diseases.

Anthracnose, circular dark spots on the leaves, and Angular Leaf Spot, water soaked spots on the leaves, can be mitigated by planting in a well drained soil and practicing infrequent, but deep watering or drip irrigation. Mosaic virus which shows up as stunted plants with mottled leaves, is carried by cucumber beetles and aphids and is spread by gardeners working in a moist garden. Keep out of the garden when it's damp and clean up any trashy corners where insects like the squash bug or cucumber beetle may winter-over. Pyrethrum or Rotenone, two organic controls, can be sprayed or dusted on plants in defense of the cucumber beetle.

Rotating squash and its relatives at least every two years will also reduce reoccurrence of insect and disease problems.

Cutworm collars, any barrier protecting the plant's stem, will discourage that pest. To be effective, the collar needs to go one inch deep into the soil and two inches above the ground.

Squash vine borers cause wilted runners and vines, and occur most often in winter squash varieties. Slitting the affected vine and removing the worm will work on a limited basis.

Aphids, whiteflies and red spider mites, those tiny critters that can create such a nuisance, enjoy squash. Yellow sticky traps and insecticidal soap sprays are often used against whiteflies and aphids. There is no good treatment for the spider mites in the home vegetable garden, except overhead watering, which seems to lessen their numbers somewhat.

BEANS

Vital Statistics

Common name:	BEANS
Botanical name:	Phaseolus vulgaris
Family:	Leguminosae (Pea Family)
Season:	warm season crop
Site:	full sun
Soil requirements:	pH 5.5-6.5, well drained, sandy loam or clay loam; moderate level of Phosphorus and Potassium, low Nitrogen requirement
Seed germination:	eight days in soil temperatures between 77 and 86 degrees, F., 80 degrees F. optimum temperature for germination
Plant size:	bush snap beans- 14 to 18 inches tall, 12 in. wide pole beans- six to ten feet long, twining vines
Days to maturity:	50-85
Plant with:	radishes, carrots, potatoes, cabbages, cucumbers, corn, strawberries, summer savory (deters bean beetle)
Avoid planting with:	onions, garlic

Roots and Rumors

The bean plant's delicate white blossoms so captivated the Conquistadors that they took the plant back to Spain for ornamental display rather than as a food.

At that time, the Europeans thought beans too intractable for civilized tongues or teeth. Once the Spaniards began cooking string beans, though, the rest of Europe followed suit.

The pods of green beans that were cultivated in the Americas for thousands of years were stringy and full of parchment. The original string bean is believed to have originated in Central America. Lima and butter beans first appeared in South America over 6,000 years ago. For the past 8,000 years, the lentil has been cultivated in the Middle East, and fava beans are from the nearby Mediterranean region.

All around the world, dried beans are the mainstay of many peoples' diets, providing a rich source of protein. By serving beans with a grain product such as corn, wheat, or rice, the daily protein requirement can be met without the addition of meat. Another positive attribute of the legumes is their ability to replenish Nitrogen to the soil. But best of all, beans are easy to grow and especially delicious fresh from the garden.

How-to

Wait until the ground is warm enough to sit on before planting beans. Otherwise, seeds may rot or the plants could suffer from damping off. Soak the seeds in water overnight before planting. Spade the soil to a depth of six to eight inches, and add a small amount of organic matter. Smooth out the seed bed and water deeply before planting. Do not water again until the beans are two inches tall to avoid crusting soil, which is impossible for bean seedlings to penetrate. Regular irrigation, providing one inch of water per week, will meet the plant's needs.

Plant bush bean seeds one inch deep, three to four inches apart in a wide row, or the same distance apart in single rows four to five inches apart. Lima beans need six inches between plants. Pole bean seeds should also be planted one inch deep, with five to six seeds around six-foot tall poles, six to eight inches away from the poles.

For a continuous, staggered crop of beans, plant in relays-adding another row of beans every two weeks.

Unless, like the early Conquistadors, you appreciate the ornamental value of the bean plant, container gardening is not recommended because of the relatively low yield per unit of space. Beans can be grown in containers with a capacity of ten gallons or more.

Snap beans are most flavorful and tender if they are harvested when they are still relatively small. Picking all mature beans every three to five days will keep production high.

Shelling beans can be harvested in three stages. While they are still young, shelling beans can be harvested and eaten like snap beans, pods and all. The second stage harvest, when beans are mature, but not dry, is best for lima and butter beans. Pods are not generally eaten at this stage, but the shelling beans are still eaten fresh and green. For soup beans, wait until the end of the season when plants and pods are completely dried up and the beans are hard.

Fresh green beans will keep in the refrigerator for up to one week, if you don't wash them first. When you've had your fill of fresh beans, try freezing a batch. First, clean the beans, trim the ends, and cut them up to the desired size. Blanch the beans by plunging them into vigorously boiling water for two to four minutes. Remove them from the hot water and dunk them into ice water. Drain, then pack them into air-tight containers.

University of California Master Gardener Bill Franklin suggests air drying beans the old fashioned Tennessee "leather britches" way. Start with an 18-inch length of string and a darning needle. Thread the needle and run it through the first seed of the snap bean. Tie a knot around the end of the first bean, then string more beans until they fill a length of 12 inches. Hang the completed strings from the house rafters outdoors or in a warm, dry spot in the house. When you're ready to make a hearty pot of soup, add a string of leather britches. Their distinctive flavor and texture will brighten up the meal.

The major categories of beans are fresh snap beans (green or string beans), and shelling or soup beans, which are shelled and dried for winter use. Some varieties grow on compact bushes while others, the "pole beans" grow as vines, twirling around strings, poles, and fences. Bush beans are the easiest to grow, requiring no staking or other support, while pole beans take up less space and often produce for a longer period of time, resulting in greater yields.

The Vermont Bean Seed Company offers over 70 different beans from all over the world, both hybrid and heritage varieties.

Problems and Solutions

Because of their shallow, fibrous root systems, beans are particularly sensitive to overwatering and strong winds. They are also sensitive to salty soils.

Anthracnose, bacterial blight, common bean mosaic virus, and rust are the most prevalent bean diseases. Anthracnose and rust, black and red blisters on the leaves, are fungus diseases that can be avoided by rotating crops, removing diseased plants from the garden, and buying certified seeds. Staying out of the garden when it is wet and establishing a well drained soil will help prevent bacterial blight, large brown spots on leaves and water soaked spots on the pods.

Common bean mosaic is a virus carried in bean seeds and spread by aphids. Buying resistant varieties and controlling aphids will avoid the mottled, curled leaves and reduced production of virus-infected plants.

Aphids, whiteflies, cutworms, cucumber beetles, harlequin bugs, stink bugs, root knot nematodes, mites, bean leaf beetles,

and the Mexican bean beetle may be found in the bean ,
They appear before blossom time, laying yellow-orange
masses on the undersides of leaves. The gardener sho.
remove the leaves and destroy the egg clusters before the,
hatch. Once adult beetles appear, rotenone, an organic pesticide can be used against them. Rotenone can also be used as
a control against the bean leaf beetle, whose damage consists
of eating large holes in the bean leaves. Resistant varieties can
lessen the destruction of soil borne root knot nematodes, and
overhead watering will keep down the number of mites in the
garden.

Peanuts

Although some children believe that the peanut, like money,
grows on trees, it is actually a subterranean member of the
legume family. Peanuts sprout their pods underground, beneath a beautiful, rich green flowering plant. They are a treat
for kids to grow, especially at harvest time.

You can start a peanut bush from any raw (unroasted)
peanut, whether purchased from a garden store, health food
store, or local supermarket. The two main varieties are the
early maturing Spanish peanut and the jumbo Virginia peanut,
which tastes better but takes a month longer to mature. Peanuts
need 100 to 120 warm days to mature fully.

Start by carefully removing the seed, keeping the red skin
intact. Soak the seeds overnight in warm water. Plant four
seeds in a mound, with mounds 18 inches apart or in rows two
feet apart.

After the plants have grown to six inches, cultivate the soil,
apply mulch, and thin to two plants per mound. Peanuts need
plenty of moisture, especially when the plants are flowering.
If the soil gets soggy, though, the peanuts may rot.

Once the plants reach one foot tall, "hill" them by pulling
the soil up around the stems. Blossoms will appear between 45
and 55 days after planting. Peanuts are ready to harvest when

the leaves turn yellow. Slowly pry the whole plant from the ground with a garden fork and shake off any loose soil. Let the peanuts dry on the plant in a shaded, warm, airy place for two to three weeks before pulling them from the plant.

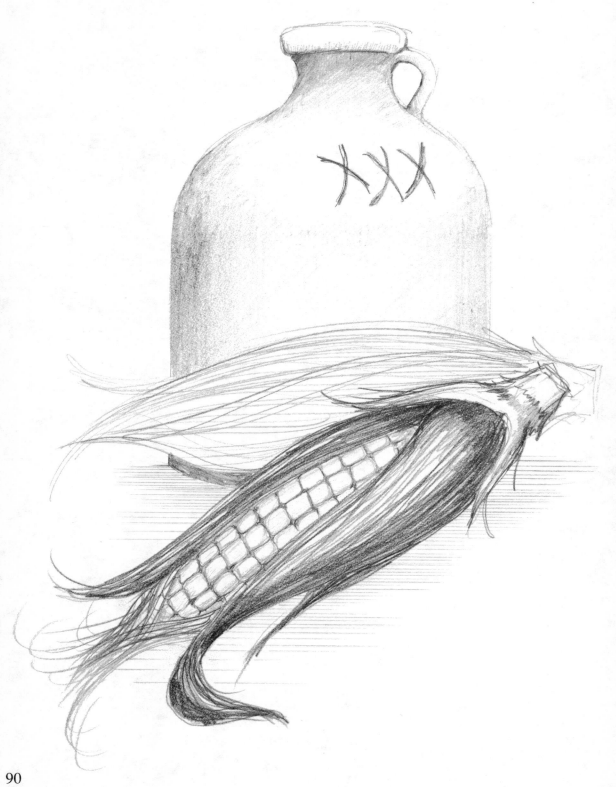

Corn

Vital Statistics

Common name:	CORN
Botanical name:	Zea mays rugosa
Family:	Gramineae (Grass family)
Season:	warm season crop
Site:	full sun
Plants per person:	15-20 corn stalks in a block minimum for good germination
Soil requirements:	pH 5.5-6.8, needs medium to heavy soil, rich with organic matter, good drainage
Seed germination:	four days at 86-95 degrees F. soil temperature, 5-7 days at 68-77 degrees F.
Plant size:	four to eight feet tall
Days to maturity:	60-120
Plant with:	potatoes, pole beans, cucumbers, pumpkins, winter squash, gourds
Avoid planting with:	tomatoes, peppers, eggplant

Roots and Rumors

The Mazola Oil commercials taught millions of Americans that the Indian word for corn is maize. The Indian translation of maize is "our life." Indeed, corn was an important crop of the Maya, Aztec and Inca civilizations, constituting the staple of their diets.

All Indians held festivals of thanksgiving for good corn harvests, human sacrifice being the final tribute to a bumper crop.

Because of its tall, proud and prolific profile, the cornstalk was a supreme deity to many early Indian tribes. Corn kernels, too, were highly regarded by the Indians. Corn kernels were placed under a brave's marriage blanket as insurance that only strong, worthy (male) offspring would issue from that union.

Although the exact origin of corn is unknown, it is believed to be a native of tropical America, cultivated as a principle food source in Mexico, Central and South America since pre-Columbian times. A discovery of fossilized maize pollen grain in Mexico dates back about 80,000 years.

In North America, corn has been an important crop ever since colonial times. This crop became especially valuable during Prohibition when back country stills pumped out gallons of corn liquor for the bootleggers' booty. Corn liquor was the source of the early American terms "corned", meaning drunk and "corny- faced", connoting a person red and pimply with drink. "Corny", derived from "corn-fed" meaning music played in the country style, out of date, hillbilly. The term was widely used by teenagers in the 1940's and 1950's, but using "corny" has now become corny in itself.

Corn-talk is slowly fading from our language, but growing corn has not lost its appeal.

> *"Heap high the farmer's wintry hoard!*
> *Heap high the golden corn!*
> *No richer gift has Autumn poured*
> *From out her lavish horn!*
>
> **John Greenleaf Whittier**

Even though corn is one of the least efficient vegetables, based upon food production per unit of garden space and unit of time, the exceptional taste of fresh picked corn was enough to inspire the poetry of Whittier and to induce many a gardener to cultivate corn.

How-to

A member of the grass family, corn is thought to have been domesticated from a wild grain. Even with a tap root that reaches three to five feet deep into the soil and auxiliary above-ground "prop roots," the tall stalks benefit from the additional support hilling soil around the base of the plants provides.

When the plants are about two-thirds grown, tassels, the male flowers, develop. Three days later silks, the female flowers, appear. If pollinated, each silk will grow into a kernel of corn.

Primary pollination occurs by wind. For this reason, choosing a spot with good air circulation and planting at least four rows side-by-side is recommended. Also, to avoid cross-pollination of sweet corn with field, ornamental, or popcorn, don't plant them in the same plot.

When choosing a spot for corn in the garden, remember that it needs full sun and also tends to shade out its neighbors. Planting corn on the north or east end of the garden will minimize that problem. Pumpkins, melons, cucumbers or gourds can be planted in the corn patch. Their wandering vines will travel unhampered through the cornstalks, covering the soil and keeping down the weeds.

Pole beans are another good companion to corn. They "fix" nitrogen in the soil, making it available to the hungry corn. In turn, corn stalks provide support for the bean vines. Plant beans two weeks after corn, one bean seed, one inch away from each corn seedling, on its south side.

Give corn plenty of water, especially once the tassels form, and also make sure nutrients are constantly available in the soil for this heavy feeder.

The Indians planted each kernel of corn above a dead fish. If you don't have any dead fish, add compost, manure, bloodmeal, alfalfa meal or a commercial fertilizer (10-10-10) to the soil before planting. Two supplemental sidedressings during the growing season should satisfy corn's hefty appetite.

Corn Crop Basics

1. Turn the soil to a depth of 6-10 inches, incorporating organic matter to satisfy this soil-demanding crop.
2. Irrigate to a depth of 3-4 feet before planting.
3. Plant seeds 1 1/2 inches deep, 8-10 inches apart, in rows 24-36 inches apart. (Plant at least 4 rows per block to insure pollination).
4. Dig furrows 6 inches deep between the rows for irrigation.
5. Cultivate the soil one inch deep around plants once they are 3 inches tall, continuing weekly until they are 30 inches tall, to control weeds.
6. Irrigate at least one foot deep every week in the summer, every 5 days on sandy soil or when it is very hot. If their leaves roll upwards, plants need more water.
7. Sidedress with nitrogen fertilizer when corn is knee high, and then again when it tassels. Apply a thin line of fertilizer (compost, manure or 10-10-10) four inches from the plants on each side of the rows. Water well.
8. Once tassels form, hill corn every 2-3 weeks by pulling soil up around the base of the plant.
9. Harvest when ears grow plump and silks dry out. Milky juice will exude from a fingernail-punctured kernel when the corn is ripe (clear juice indicates immaturity). Harvest the ear with a sharp, downward twist. (Wait until stalks and leaves are completely dry to harvest popcorn or ornamental varieties.)

10.Eat or freeze as soon after harvest as possible, following Mark Twain's adage: "Boil a pot of water in the field and shuck the ears into it."

For late varieties, try planting corn Indian-style, in a round, slightly raised mound with stalks 10-12 inches apart. Before fall wind and rain begins, wrap twine around the mound's outer corn stalks for support.

Because of its size and soil requirements, corn is not a practical plant for container growing.

Problems and Solutions

The two major corn diseases, root rot and corn smut, can be avoided through good cultural practices. The stunted plants that result from root rot will not occur if the gardener waits until the soil is warm enough to plant, and if the soil is well drained. Corn smut, spongy galls on corn ears, is caused by a soil fungus and can be discouraged by rotating crops.

The most troublesome pest of the corn field is the corn earworm. Dipel or Attack can be used against the earworm, or mineral oil dropped into each ear after the silks start to dry out, but both treatments are rather tedious. The purple-brown worm doesn't become a serious problem until mid-August, so early varieties often escape damage. If the gardener is planting early and late varieties, most of the early harvests could be used for freezing and the later ones, if the cornworm moves in, can be trimmed and used for fresh consumption.

Corn on the cob is easy to freeze. Husk and wash the ears, scald small ears for 6 minutes, large ears for 10 minutes, then cool in ice water for the same length of time. After draining the cobs, pack them in freezer containers or bags, seal, label and freeze. To cook, place unthawed cob in cool water, bring to a boil and cook for 5-10 minutes.

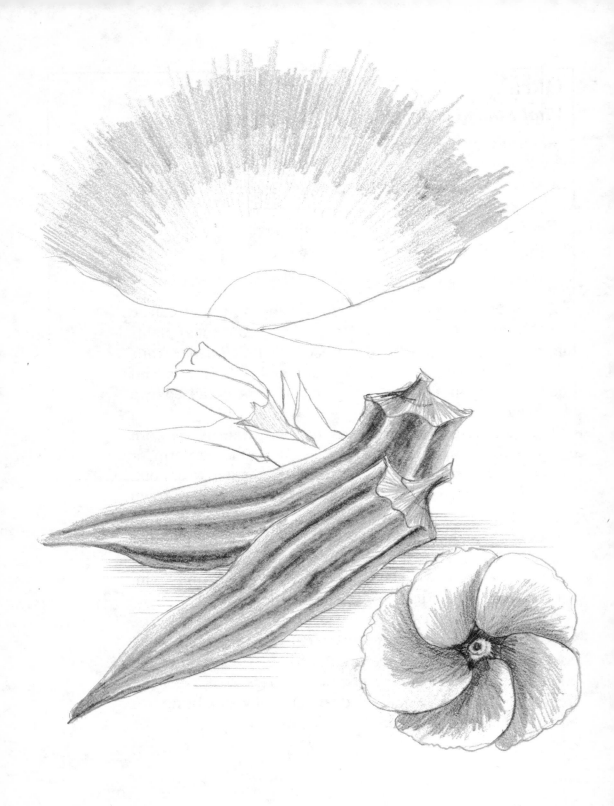

Okra

Vital Statistics

Common name:	OKRA
Botanical name:	Abelmoschus esculentus
Family:	Hibiscus
Season:	Warm season crop
Site:	full sun
Plants per person:	eight to ten
Soil requirements:	pH 6- 6.9, add only moderate amount of organic matter
Seed germination:	6-7 days at soil temperature between 86 and 104 degrees Fahrenheit, 12-17 days at 68- 77 degrees
Plant size:	three to six feet tall
Days to maturity:	56
Plant with:	squash, cucumbers, beans, lettuce
Avoid planting with:	corn, tomatoes, peppers, eggplant

Roots and Rumors

In the Deep South, okra is still know as "slave fruit." African slaves receive credit for bringing this unusual crop to the New World.

The actual origin of okra remains a mystery, but wild varieties have been found in Ethiopia and Sudan. Ancient Arab physicians called okra pods "sun vessels" because of their dramatic flowering habit. The pale yellow petals deepen in color as the sun rises, flaring open to reveal a crimson heart, usually right at sunset.

Many primitive people swore by the curative power of okra seeds which, once consumed, were believed to float through the body forever.

Today, okra is a basic ingredient of gumbo, its distinctive flavor and texture being hard to miss. Some people consider it too slimy to eat, but others love this vegetable fried, pickled, stewed, or fresh from the garden.

How-to

A member of the hibiscus family, okra grows on upright, spike-leafed plants with pods pointing sharply from the stem into the sky.

Okra loves the heat, preferring a temperature range of 65 to 95 degrees, F.

By soaking the seeds in warm water for 24 hours or putting them in the freezer overnight before planting, the hard seed cover will crack, speeding up germination.

A good spacing for okra is one seed, one-half inch deep, every three to four inches in rows 12 to 18 inches apart. Watering is best done after seeds are planted and the soil has been firmly patted back into place. When the plants begin to blossom and then again a month later, sidedress with a balanced fertilizer.

Okra should be picked every day (using a sharp knife and wearing gloves to prevent itchiness) as the young pods reach three to four inches in length. They can be stored in the refrigerator from 8-10 days.

Clemson Spineless, the most popular okra variety, will grow to six feet high. This variety is available in almost every seed catalog. Some three-foot dwarf varieties are now available.

Problems and Solutions

It isn't often that the okra plant is attacked by insects or diseases. Aphids, corn earworms, stink bugs, and nematodes, however, on occasion frequent okra plantings. A soapy water spray or malathion can be used against aphids; Attack or Dipel will discourage the earworm. Stinkbugs should be hand-picked from the okra plants and the only protection from nematodes is resistant varieties.

The only major disease of okra in California is wilt. The affected plants wilt, then collapse completely, with the stem tissue showing a dark brown discoloration under the bark. There is no cure for this fungal disease, and no resistant okra varieties as yet.

Carrots

Vital Statistics

Common name:	CARROTS AND PARSNIPS
Botanical name:	Daucus carota
Family name:	Umbelliferae (Parsley Family)
Season:	cool season crop
Site:	needs full sun or partial shade
Plants per person:	50-75
Soil requirements:	pH 5.5-6.8, loose, sandy soil, lots of organic matter
Seed germination:	one to two weeks
Plant size:	carrot tops 10-16 inches tall
Days to maturity:	60-85
Plant with:	radishes, peas, leaf lettuce, chives, onions, tomatoes
Avoid planting with:	dill

Roots and Rumors

Carrots as an aphrodisiac? Over the centuries myths about the sensual power of carrots accompanied their varied and sundry medicinal remedies, preceding their eventual use as food and fodder.

They probably originated in Afghanistan as a purple root. Carrot cultivars range in color from white to yellow, orange, red purple, and black. The early Afghanistani purple variety was domesticated around 600 A.D. and distributed through Europe and the Middle East during the eighth, ninth and tenth centuries.

During the ninth or tenth century a yellow mutant of the purple cultivar was discovered and cultivated in Syria or Iran. Yellow carrots reached the south of Spain in the eleventh century and spread to the rest of Europe by the fourteenth century.

In Holland during the seventeenth century, an orange mutant arose which quickly caught on because of its ability to retain its color after cooking. The Dutch began to feed carrots to their Holstein cows, producing their famous rich yellow butter and cheese which is still popular today.

By the eighteenth century, orange carrots had been distributed all over the world. The first settlers at Jamestown, Virginia brought carrot seeds. Their carrot crop helped save them from starvation in the winter of 1609. Soon after, carrots were being grown by the American Indians.

Carrots are popular because they are inexpensive, easily grown, good shippers, and boast a long storage life and high nutritive value. Long praised as a rich source of Vitamin A, carrots have recently been recognized as a cancer preventive agent in humans because of their carotene content.

How-to

A member of the Umbelliferae Family, so named because of the umbrella-shaped foliage of family members, the carrot is related to celery, chervil, parsley, anise, fennel, parsnip, coriander, caraway, cumin, dill, lovage, Queen Anne's Lace, and poison hemlock.

The basic requirements for producing good carrots are having a loose, well drained soil fortified with bone meal or superphosphate; regular, deep watering; and diligent weeding and thinning.

The month of August is carrot sowing time for a fall harvest, while mid-February is the ideal planting time for a spring crop in the valleys. However, carrot seeds can be sown any time from the end of January through the middle of April.

The easiest way to start carrots is to broadcast the seeds over the surface of a well-cultivated bed, then gently rake them into the soil. A shade cloth is required to protect seedlings from the summer sun and reduce the soil temperature to a degree low enough for germination when plants are started in August. For two weeks after sowing seeds, spring carrots should be protected from heavy rains by covering them with a clear plastic sheet. Carrot seeds can take up to three weeks to germinate.

Once carrots reach one inch in diameter, thin them to two inches apart. Remove weeds regularly.

When carrot greens turn a deep, dark color, they are ready to harvest. Hairy carrots are the result of too much nitrogen. Forked or twisted carrots develop in heavy or compacted soil. The addition of organic matter will help prevent this problem. Also, the shorter varieties of carrots, such as Nantes Half Long or Danvers Half Long, usually fare better than the longer varieties in a heavy soil.

The shorter varieties also make excellent container plants. For such culture, choose a container 8 to 12 inches deep with drainage holes, and fill with a loose, rich soil mix. A 7-gallon tub will produce 10-15 mature carrots. Thin carrots to two inches apart, paying close attention to watering and providing at least eight hours of sunlight or artificial light.

Fresh young carrots are deliciously refreshing straight out

of the garden. Tender carrot greens from the thinnings are also a flavorful addition to spring salads, similar in taste to parsley.

Fall plantings can be stored in the ground over the winter. Carrots will keep in the refrigerator for several months.

Parsnips, also known as "white carrots" have similar cultural requirements. They have a longer growing period - no less than four months - and require 18 inches of loose, rich soil.

Problems and Solutions

The only significant pest of the carrot is the root maggot. One way to overcome them is to plant radishes nearby to act as a trap, attracting the maggots away from the carrots.

Rotating crops (not planting carrots in the same spot for more than three years) and buying good seed should prevent common carrot disease.

Beets, Spinach, Swiss Chard

Vital Statistics

Common name:	BEETS, SPINACH, SWISS CHARD
Botanical name:	Beta vulgaris
Family:	Chenopodiaceae (Goosefoot Family, includes spinach, chard, and tumble weed)
Season:	Cool season crop
Site:	full sun or light shade
Plants per person:	40-50
Soil requirements:	pH 6.0-6.8, sandy loam or well drained clay loam, lots of organic matter
Seed germination:	five days at 77-86 degrees F. soil temperature (when presoaked or presprouted)
Plant size:	greens 12-18 inches tall
Days to maturity:	50-70
Plant with:	onions, kohlrabi, radishes, turnips
Avoid planting with:	pole beans

Roots and Rumors

Beets and spinach are probably the two vegetables most shunned by children. Even some adults gag at the mention of beets. Why this aversion exists is a real mystery.

These much maligned cousins, beets, spinach and chard are members of the Goosefoot Family. The garden beet is believed to have descended from the sea beet which is indigenous to southern Europe.

Raised for its greens long before the roots were consumed, the beet was cultivated back to the fourth century, B.C. The ancient Greeks broke with tradition and served up both the leaves and roots of beets.

Invading armies spread the beet to northern Europe. German gardeners further refined the garden beet during the thirteenth century, and also developed the mangel wurzel, a larger, coarse, white-fleshed variety grown primarily as fodder for livestock.

Herbalist Gerard proclaimed in his seventeenth century writing: "The great and beautiful beet may be used in winter for a sallad herb, with vinegar, oyle, and salt, and is not only pleasant to the taste, but also delightful to the eye."

Swiss chard probably evolved from the beet and is actually a beet top without the edible root.

Spinach originated in central Asia. The Persians first cultivated spinach to feed their treasured cats. The Persian word for spinach, isfanakh, means green hand.

During the sixth century, spinach traveled from Persia to China where they called it "Persian herbs." The Chinese planted spinach extensively along the outer fringe of their rice fields. They eventually took spinach to India and Nepal where it became known as "China flower."

By the twelfth century, the Moors had introduced spinach to Spain, and within 100 years it became known in the rest of Europe as "Spanish green."

Of this well-traveled green with many names, the Medes

prescribed washing every leaf of spinach that went into a pot twelve times - eleven in water were meant to "free the vegetable of its dark, earthy associations." The twelfth, in human tears, was to season it "with God's wisdom."

How-to

Beets. Ideally suited to small spaces, beets can be planted as a border in flower beds, squeezed in between other vegetables, or cultivated as a colorful container crop. While most varieties are frost hardy, beet seedlings cannot endure extreme heat. Fall plantings should be protected from the sun with a shade cloth.

Beets prosper in a light sandy loam, well fortified with manure or a commercial fertilizer prior to planting. An extra sidedressing of a balanced fertilizer when plants are two to four inches tall will give them an extra boost.

If the soil is heavy clay or lacks good drainage, the gardener may choose to grow beets in a raised bed or in a container. An efficient and attractive container crop, beets two to three inches apart in a shallow three to seven gallon tub will produce a healthy harvest.

To speed up germination, soak seeds in lukewarm water for three hours before planting.

They can be grown in rows 10 inches apart, planted 1/2 inch deep in the soil, or seeds can be broadcasted sparingly over a wide bed. Once seedlings reach 1/4 to 1/2 inch tall, they should be thinned to 1 to 2 inches apart. The next thinnings, spacing plants 2 to 3 inches apart, produce edible greens perfect for salads or steaming.

Beets need a constantly moist seed bed to sprout seedlings, and then deep watering to promote good tap roots. Lack of moisture could prevent germination or result in tough stringy beets. Mulching will help retain moisture and moderate soil temperature.

Beets with the thickest stems produce the biggest roots.

Once the root reaches the size of a golf ball, harvest may begin.

Pull out the entire plant while it is still young, tender, and flavorful. Fall plantings can be stored in the ground over the winter. Beets will keep in the refrigerator for up to two weeks.

To reduce bleeding when cooking, leave one inch of the leaf stalk attached to the root and do not cut the root at all until after it is cooked.

Problems and Solutions

Root maggots, aphids, earwigs, snails, slugs, and rodents, particularly gophers, attack beets, but they suffer no serious disease problems. Root maggots can be drawn away from beets by planting radishes nearby as a lure. A soapy water spray, yellow sticky trap, or an application of Malathion can be used to control aphids. Earwigs eat aphids, but sometimes also eat beet greens. To trap earwigs, set a wooden slat, a short length of hose, or rolled up newspaper near the crop, disposing of the earwigs each morning. Snails and slugs love the smell of beer and are easily drowned in a shallow bowl of it set out in the garden. Many baits and traps are also available to control these pests. Gophers are harder to eliminate. Hardware screening placed in the soil under root crops is sometimes the only way to keep the gophers out. Gopher traps are also available.

"Zoning," white rings around the beet, is caused by wide variations in moisture or nutrients. Deep, regular irrigation and the application of a mulch can reduce chances of experiencing this problem.

Spinach and Swiss Chard

A fall planting of spinach in October will be ready for harvest in May. A complementary spring planting of Swiss chard, between mid-February and March will keep the gardener in greens from May through November.

Spinach tends to bolt (go to seed) in hot weather, so fall plantings are best in the valleys. Chard, on the other hand, is a biennial plant which often goes to seed in the spring, if planted in the fall, but is heat tolerant. Soil requirements for spinach and chard are the same as beets, but chard is less particular, thriving in almost any soil. Insect and disease problems are minimal, as with beets.

Both spinach and chard make excellent container crops. Spinach is often planted with later maturing vegetables, while three healthy chard plants can fill an entire three gallon container on their own.

Spinach can be grown in rows, or preferrably in a wide bed with seeds two inches apart. Start thinning when leaves are barely big enough to eat, with plants eventually spaced 6 to 12 inches apart.

Chard grows well in rows 18 to 24 inches apart with seeds planted 2 to 3 inches apart, 1/2 inch deep. Mature plants should stand 8 to 10 inches apart.

Spinach is usually harvested by pulling the whole plant from the soil while chard is often harvested leaf by leaf, providing a heavy and sustained crop of greens for months. Both are highly perishable - chard can be refrigerated for 2 to 3 days, spinach for up to five days.

Radishes

Vital Statistics

Common name:	RADISHES
Botanical name:	Raphanus sativus
Family:	Cruciferae (Mustard Family)
Season:	Cool season crop
Site:	full sun or partial shade
Plants per person:	40-50
Soil requirements:	5.5-6.8 pH, early crops - sandy or silty loam, later crops - heavier soils
Seed germination:	three days at 77-86 degrees F. soil temperature, four to six days at 59-68
Plant size:	one inch to 30 pounds
Days to maturity:	salad varieties: 3-4 weeks, winter radishes: 50-70 days
Plant with:	peas, lettuce, cucumbers, carrots, cabbage, beets, onions
Avoid planting with:	no known enemies

Roots and Rumors

"For breakfast, dinner and supper, three times a day, they are a most appetizing and wholesome relish." So suggests Burpee's 1888 catalog along with its listing of 17 varieties of radishes.

In the United States, we most often think of radishes as a condiment, cultivating the bunching varieties or salad types for fresh consumption. "Keeping radishes," the long, fat, turnip- like varieties were a staple in Europe during the Middle Ages and today are very important crops in Asia. In Japan, the daikon radish was ranked first in 1974 among all vegetables grown. Also known as "winter radishes," these giant roots are cooked or pickled, along with their leaves.

Botanists are not sure where radishes originated. Some believe it was China, others think it was the eastern Mediterranean region.

From inscriptions on the walls of pyramids, it is apparent that radishes were an important food crop in Egypt since about 2000 B.C.

Radishes were also valuable to the ancient Greeks. A physician named Moschian wrote an entire book about them.

How-to

Salad radishes are fast and easy to grow, and meet many needs in the garden. They can be grown any time of the year, but watch out for radishes planted in the heat of summer, as the heat is captured in their taste.

No special soil treatment is necessary for the small radish varieties, but winter radishes need a deep, manure-enriched bed.

Overcrowding is a common problem with radishes. Salad radishes should be thinned to one-and-a-half inches apart, winter radishes 4-6 inches apart.

Radishes should be harvested before they turn spongy and pithy. They can be stored in the refrigerator for up to two weeks.

Because they germinate so quickly, gardeners plant radishes beside slow germinating crops, such as carrots and beets, to mark the rows. They are also planted near other root crops, such as onions and turnips, to act as a decoy, drawing root maggots, leaf hoppers and flea beetles from other plants. Since they repel cucumber beetles and spider mites, radishes are good companions for melons, squash, and cucumbers.

Problems and Solutions

Radishes suffer, usually to a much lesser degree, from the same insects that attack their cabbage cousins. They grow so quickly, though, that if one planting becomes infested by anything, the gardener can pull up and dispose of them and start fresh in another spot of the garden. Likewise, diseases don't usually have a chance to set in before harvest time arrives.

Bolting, producing a flower stalk before the root can mature, is a common problem when radishes are planted in warm weather.

Windowsill Salad Bowl

Radishes are seldom eaten alone, but usually as a garnish or condiment with the meal. So, too, in the garden the radish is a perfect accent to other vegetables and herbs.

A combination of radishes, short carrots, leaf lettuce and onions grown indoors in a planter box or other container can brighten up the salad bowl all winter. Here's how to set up your own salad bar garden:

1. Find a container (clay, plastic, wood, styrofoam, or whatever you have) that is at least 6-8 inches deep, with drainage holes on the bottom.
2. Fill the container with artificial soil (such as Terra Lite) or a light potting soil.

3. Water well before planting, keeping soil moist but not soggy.
4. Sprinkle radish, carrot, and lettuce seeds lightly over the soil surface. Mix different varieties of each crop to lengthen harvest and add zest.
5. Cover the seeds gently with 1/4 to 1/2 inches of soil.
6. Poke the onion sets into the soil every few inches and cover lightly with soil. Green onions will be ready in three weeks.
7. Fertilize every week with a commercial liquid fertilizer.
8. Provide sufficient light, at least 6 hours, either from a window or through artificial light. If seedlings stretch toward the light source, you need more.
9. Harvest as salad reaches maturity. Reseed as desired.

Lettuce

Vital Statistics

Common name:	LETTUCE
Botanical name:	Lactuca sativa
Family:	Compositae (Sunflower)
Season:	Cool season crop
Site:	full sun spring & fall, shade from summer sun
Plants per person:	8-10
Soil requirements:	well drained soil, rich with organic matter
Seed germination:	two days at 77-86 degrees F., three days at 59-68 degrees (soil temp.) (needs light for full seed germination)
Plant size:	two to ten inches wide
Days to maturity:	10-80
Plant with:	carrots, onions, beans, tomatoes, corn, radishes cabbages, cucumbers

Roots and Rumors

Lactuca serriola, the granddaddy of the lettuces, grew wild in Asia, Eurasia and the Mediterranean region. The early Sumarians, Egyptians, Greeks and Romans were the first to appreciate the juicy leaf. During springtime festivals in Greece, pots of lettuce were ceremoniously paraded through the streets.

The Egyptians showered their fertility god Min with offerings of lettuce. They and the Assyrians believed the milky lettuce juice had aphrodisiacal properties.

Since very ancient times, lettuce was used in many cultures as a tranquilizer to induce sleep.

It was the Romans who bred the head lettuce. They were so fond of lettuce that Emperor Caesar Augustus erected a statue to the leafy greens.

John Winthrop Jr. brought lettuce seed packets from England to America in the 1600's. Salads didn't come into vogue in the United States until the twentieth century because of the effete and sissified image lettuce-based salads held. Now even "real men" eat salad.

How-to

"Lettuce is like conversation: it must be fresh and crisp, so sparkling that you scarcely notice the bitter in it," so claimed Charles Dudley Warner in the late 1800's.

Growing sweet and tender lettuce in the inland valleys of California can be a challenge. This is quite ironic, considering our proximity to the primary head lettuce producing area of the nation, California's coastline. The main cause of bitter, limp lettuce, though, is hot weather, and we get plenty of that. The key to successful lettuce cultivation is planting it early in the spring or fall, and supplying ample water and nutrients for rapid growth. Enriching the top two to three inches of soil (the area occupied by lettuce's shallow roots) with organic matter and a sidedressing of a high Nitrogen organic or commercial fertilizer will provide the necessary nutrients.

The four major types of lettuces are: looseleaf, crisphead (iceburg or head lettuce), butter head and cos or Romaine. Crisphead lettuces are best suited for cool coastal climates. The looseleafs are ideal for spring plantings while butterheads and cos do well in the fall.

There are several methods for planting lettuce. You can plant it in wide rows (12-15 inches). Broadcast the seed as evenly as possible over the entire bed. Mix the seed with sand before broadcasting to make the sowing thinner and more even. Cover the seed lightly with no more than 1/4 inch of soil, remembering that lettuce seeds uniquely require a little light for germination. Use an iron rake to thin the lettuce bed, or thin by hand. Harvest when leaves are still young and tender to avoid bitterness.

Lettuce is one of those crops that can be squeezed in between other plants in the bed. Leaf lettuces, particularly Black Seeded Simpson and Oakleaf, are naturals for this type of cultivation. Scatter the seeds under pole beans, between corn rows, around broccoli and young pepper plants and throughout the flower beds. For people with a limited planting area, this works best and provides shade for the plants as the days heat up and their neighbors' canopy of leaves unfold.

If the gardener has absolutely no ground space, lettuce makes an excellent container crop. A one-gallon container will hold two to three looseleaf lettuces or one to two butter-head or Cos. A three to five gallon container is the ideal size, allowing the gardener to mix different colors of lettuces in the same pot, or to plant lettuces with herbs or flowers for an attractive edible display.

Harvest lettuce when the leaves are still young and tender.

Once harvested, lettuce can be stored in the refrigerator for up to five days.

Problems and Solutions

Poor lettuce harvest usually results from too much, too late, or too close plantings. Be stingy while broadcasting lettuce seeds, and thin them with a passion, enjoying the tiny thinnings in your gourmet salads.

By rotating crops, controlling insects, promoting fast and vigorous growth, staying out of the garden when it is wet, and removing any diseased plants upon first discovering them, most lettuce diseases can be avoided. Anthracnose and leaf blights are the predominant lettuce diseases. Some resistant varieties are available, and seeds can be treated with a fungicide before planting if anthracnose is a severe problem.

Pests that are fond of the lettuce leaf include aphids, leafhoppers, cutworms, cabbage loopers, leaf miners, snails and slugs. A soapy spray will usually dislodge aphids. Controlling weeds around lettuce will help reduce leafhoppers and leaf miner populations.

Cutworm collars are not very practical for lettuce plants, but if cutworms are present in large numbers, collars may be necessary.

Attack or Dipel can be used against cabbage loopers. Snails and slugs love lettuce and should be trapped or eliminated as much as possible before planting the seeds.

Birds, too, love to peck at fresh new lettuce leaves. Netting or twigs scattered over the bed are often used to protect seedlings from flying flocks.

Gourmet Greens

Would you spend five dollars for a head of lettuce? Probably not, but some New York City gourmets have become accustomed to paying such prices for the succulent leaves of radicchio (rad-EEK-ee-o), imported from Italy for dinner salads.

Also known as red-leaf chicory, radicchio has been a popular salad green and cooked vegetable throughout Europe for centuries. The tangy, slightly bitter tasting, bright red-to-bronze maroon leaves are attractive, tender additions to any salad bowl.

The radicchio rage has caught on along the West Coas
but with our Mediterranean climate so similar to that of
we can grow our own instead of paying the inflated pric
imported produce.

Since the plant is extremely cold hearty, foothill resic
as well as valley dwellers can cultivate radicchio. It also
well in the greenhouse or as a container plant.

The chicories do best when planted in July or August (or as
late as September for a spring crop), spacing plants 10-12
inches apart with rows 18 inches apart. Seeds will sprout in
four to ten days.

Keep an eye out for snails during the entire growing period.
Insects are seldom a problem, but occasionally rabbits will
gnaw on the leaves.

Seedlings grow vigorously, with bright green leaves at first.
Leaves will become splotchy brown, then turn red with cool
weather.

Harvest through winter and early spring as color intensifies
and the flavor of the inner leaves becomes mild. Cut off a head
and trim it as you would a cabbage, leaving the stem and a few
leaves to form secondary heads.

Peas

Vital Statistics

Common name:	PEAS
Botanical name:	Pisum sativum
Family:	Leguminosae
Season:	Cool season crop
Site:	needs full sun
Plants per person:	50-60
Soil requirements:	5.5-6.8 pH, well drained clay loam with good organic matter content. Will grow in sandy soils, but less productive.
Seed germination:	six days at 77-86 degrees F. soil temperature, seven to nine days at 59-68 degrees
Plant size:	vines from 12 inches to over 5 feet
Days to maturity:	55-75
Plant with:	carrots, turnips, radishes, cucumbers, corn, beans
Avoid planting with:	onions, garlic, potatoes

Roots and Rumors

The Chinese believe that Emperor Shen Nung, the "Father of Agriculture," discovered the pea and brought it into cultivation 5000 years ago, along with rice and wheat. After collecting plant material he thought suitable for cultivation, Nung would first serve it to a dog, then a servant before proclaiming it safe for popular consumption.

Most botanists agree that the pea originated in middle Asia and expanded to India through Afghanistan. A secondary area of origin is believed to be in the Near East, and a third in the plateau and mountain ranges of Ethiopia.

Primitive pea seeds dating back to the Bronze Age (3000 B.C.) were discovered in areas inhabited by Swiss lake dwellers. Excavation of the ruins of Troy and tombs of Egypt also unearthed early pea varieties.

Norse legend asserts that Thor, the thunder god, gave peas to man as punishment. When he became angry with man, he sent flying dragons to drop peas on the earth. Some of the peas fell into wells, contaminating the water. Others landed on fertile soil, providing a new crop. Grateful mortals dedicated the pea to Thor, and in his honor, ate peas only on his day, Thursday.

Ancient peas grew on vines up to eight feet long, had smooth skinned, starchy seeds, and were used as dried peas, rather than as a fresh vegetable.

During the Middle Ages, peas became a winter staple in Northern Europe.

> *"Peas porridge hot,*
> *Peas porridge cold,*
> *Peas porridge in the pot*
> *Nine days old."*

This old English nursery rhyme began in the days when peas porridge, a dish similar to split pea soup, filled the bowls of peasants on a daily basis.

By the end of the seventeenth century, the Dutch introduced

a new, sweet variety and took it to France where it was named "petit pois."

Mme. de Maintenon of the French court wrote in 1696: *"The impatience to eat them, the pleasure of having eaten them, and the joy of eating them again are the three points of private gossip . . . it is both a fashion and a madness."*

Columbus planted peas in Santo Domingo in 1492, and they were quickly adopted by American Indians. Thomas Jefferson's favorite vegetable was the pea. He listed 50 varieties in his *Garden Book.*

Dwarf varieties appeared in the 1800's. Soon wrinkled seeded varieties made their debut, quickly overshadowing their starchier, smooth skinned cousins. Only one smooth seeded garden pea variety, the Alaska, remains viable commercially today. Several of the most popular varieties of wrinkled skinned garden peas - Little Marvel, Alderman, and Telephone were introduced between 1880 and 1900.

The most recent development in wrinkled skinned pea propagation occurred in 1979. That year the Sugar Snap edible podded snap pea was named as the All American selection. Gardeners everywhere fell in love with this new variety whose pod walls are thicker than the snow peas, but edible during immature stages.

How-to

Peas thrive in cooler climates. A few spring days of hot weather can paralyze pea production. Late October through November is the best time to plant peas in the valleys.

They are sensitive to wind and all except the dwarf varieties require support.

Peas don't like to "get their feet wet," so good drainage is important. For this reason, raised beds are ideal sites to grow peas. They require plenty of calcium and magnesium, which will be present if a healthy helping of compost or other organic matter is worked into the soil prior to planting. No other fertilization will be required. In fact, peas are good soil builders, taking nitrogen from the air and bringing it into the soil, then converting it chemically to a form usable by other plants.

Before planting, cultivate the top 12 inches of soil and water to a depth of four feet. Withhold water until plants are at least three inches tall.

On a wide bed, peas can be scattered one to two inches apart, one inch deep in the soil. If planted in rows, dwarf varieties need two feet between rows, regular vining varieties need three feet between rows with plants thinned to two inches apart.

Once the young seedlings pop through the soil, they become prime targets for pea-loving birds. Protect them with netting or twigs for a week or two.

Because of their sensitivity to wind, find a protected corner for planting, if possible. Peas can be grown in containers, but it is not recommended because of their relatively low production rate. If you're not too concerned about yield per square inch, with proper support, peas do make an attractive container crop. Careful watering is a must.

When pea pods begin to bulge but are still bright green and velvety, it's harvest time. Garden peas should be harvested every week, sugar peas every two to three days. Harvesting all mature pods regularly will keep the plants producing vigorously.

Refrigeration will keep peas fresh for up to five days after harvest, but fresh picked peas are the most flavorful and tender.

Problems and Solutions

Pea aphids and weevils are the only significant enemies of peas. These are not common problems in California, though. Some gardeners plant spearmint or garlic near peas to discourage these insects or use a lightly soapy spray to dislodge them from the plants. Pyrethrum or rotenone, two biological insecticides, can be used against the pea aphid, or malathion is the chemical control. Rotenone and malathion are also effective against the pea weevil.

Mildew is a common problem with peas. Well drained soil, crop rotation and the selection of disease resistant varieties and seeds treated with a fungicide can reduce the incidence of mildew.

By far the most significant problems of cultivating peas are pod set failure, due to unexpected spring heat, and the pea plant's natural inclination to dry up and die once summer arrives.

Onions

Vital Statistics

Common name:	ONIONS, CHIVES, SHALLOTS, GARLIC, LEEKS
Botanical name:	Allium cepa
Family:	Amaryllidaceae (Amaryllis family)
Season:	cool season crop
Site:	needs full sun
Plants per person:	6-12 Egyptian onions 30-40 green onions 25 fresh bulbs 50-100 for drying onions
Soil requirements:	pH 5.5-6.5, prefer sandy loam or heavier soils with plenty of organic matter
Seed germination:	three to four days at 70-80 degrees, F., soil temperature
Plant size:	greens 10-12 inches tall
Days to maturity:	90-250
Plant with:	beets, strawberries, tomatoes, lettuce
Avoid planting with:	peas, beans

Roots and Rumors

The onion family probably sprouted up in central Asia over 5,000 years ago. In Asia, people considered the onion an absolute divinity, erecting temples where onions bloomed. The onion was considered too celestial for human consumption in Asia and also in Egypt, where they saw the onion as a symbol of the universe and eternity because of its spherical shape.

Roman satirist Juvenal jested: "It is a sacralige to bite the leek or onion, O holy nation, in whose garden divinities spring up," mocking the Egyptians for their glorification of this root crop.

The Romans and Greeks were not without their own onion unctions. Greek medics advised males to consume one onion the size of a fist in the morning and one the size of a thumb at bedtime to lighten the balance of the blood.

The breakfast of champions during Julius Caesar's rule consisted of nothing but onions. One hundred years later, gladiators were massaged with onion juice before entering the Forum to keep their bodies firm and perhaps to lessen slightly the lions' appetites.

By the Middle Ages, onions had reached northern Europe. The word onion comes from Middle English "unyun" which is derived from the Latin "unus." Unus means one and goes back to the early association of onions as the symbol of the universe.

Until recently, the leek was the national plant of Wales. It has been replaced by the daffodil in that spot of honor, but the leek is still worn on Saint David's Day in Wales to commemorate their leek-wreathed soldiers' victory over the Saxons in 640 A.D.

Garlic, too, has been the source of many legends over the years. One Mohammedan legend traces garlic back to Creation, claiming that when Satan walked from the Garden of Eden, a garlic sprouted wherever his left foot struck the ground, an onion from his right.

The Codex Ebers, an Egyptian medical papyrus dating to around 1550 B.C. listed 22 garlic formulae to cure ailments from headaches to throat tumors. Another ancient papyrus recommended the use of garlic to determine fertility: "You shall let a clove of garlic remain the whole night in her womb until dawn. If the smell is present in her mouth, then she will conceive; if not, she will not conceive."

The Roman naturalist Pliny devised 61 garlic-based remedies, one of which was taking garlic with wine to relieve the "sting of hemorrhoid."

Gilroy, California has become the Garlic Capitol of the world. Every year local residents open up their community for the Gilroy Garlic Festival. Events include crowning of the Garlic Queen, a Great Garlic Recipe Cook-off, and the Love-That-Garlic Tennis Tournament.

How-to

The onion is a welcome addition to any garden, as best expressed by Robert Lewis Stevenson in his poem "To a Gardener":

> Let first the onion flourish there,
> Rose among the roots, the maidenfair
> Wine-scented and poetic soul
> Of the capacious salad bowl.

Bulbing onions, bunching onions (otherwise known as green onions, spring onions, scallions, or green tails), chives, shallots, garlic, leeks, and Egyptian onions are all members of the Amaryllis Family.

They appreciate a sandy loam soil, rich with organic matter and fortified with bonemeal. Being heavy feeders, bulbing onions especially thrive with two side dressings of compost, poultry manure, or a commercial fertilizer (5-10-10).

Starting from seedlings is the easiest way to grow bulbing onions, although they can be grown from seeds or sets. To plant seedlings, trim the tops back, space them three inches apart in rows 12 inches apart, and cover with soil to one half inch above the green portion of the onion.

Onions should be weeded and thinned regularly to promote bulb growth. The thinnings can be eaten or transplanted. Production of bulbs depends primarily upon day length, with "short day" varieties bulbing with 12 hours of light, "long day" varieties with 15 to 16 hours. Loosen the soil around onions once bulbs begin to swell, and mulch them well to avoid sunburn.

After the winter rains ease up, they need steady irrigation; and then none at all once a quarter of the tops have fallen over.

When that happens, about six months after planting, the onions will be ready to harvest. Uprooted onions can be dried outdoors on the ground for a few days with the tops covering the bulbs to protect them from sunburn. Once the tops are dry, they can be braided and hung in a well ventilated place, or stored in a mesh bag. Onions must be mature and thoroughly dry before storing.

Green onions can be grown from seed, or more easily from sets (small dry onion bulbs). My dad had an "onion stick," an old broom handle, that he would use to poke holes in the soil throughout the vegetable and flower beds. After he punched a small hole, he would drop in an onion set and push the soil over it with his stick. His casual onion pokings produced a constant, staggered crop of fresh green onions, a great advantage since they are highly perishable, keeping in the refrigerator for only three to five days.

Shallots, similar to green onions but with a flavor that is often described as a cross between onions and garlic, are also started from sets. Space them four to six inches apart in wide rows and feed them heavily.

Leeks, those fat green onions with a distinctive yet mild taste are most often grown from seed. With a 130 to 150 day growing period, fall plantings are the best for leeks, as with all onions in our area.

Chives are the slender members of the onion family, most commonly found chopped atop baked potatoes. They can be grown in pots on a windowsill or in any small corner of the garden. Started from seed, they sprout up and are ready for harvest within four weeks. Simply snip off the tops as needed and they will grow back in strength. If you let a few go to seed, they will come back again next year. Chinese chives have a delicious mild garlic flavor that is great in salads.

True garlic is started from cloves, broken off the bulb right before planting. They can be spaced three to four inches apart in wide rows, or scattered throughout the garden like green onions. Many rose gardeners swear by planting garlic near their rose bushes to keep insects away.

Egyptian onions, often called "walking onions," because they grow their petite purple bulbets on top of their green stalks are also easy growers. The hardest part is finding sets to get started, but once a patch is established, the gardener will have Egyptian onions, either bulbs, greens, or top bulbs, ready to harvest practically any time of the year.

All onions can be grown in containers, and are often interplanted with lettuce, radishes, and carrots for salad gardens. Usually container grown onions are harvested for their greens rather than their bulbs.

Problems and Solutions

The onion maggot is a white, worm-like creature about one-third inch long which eats at the base of the onion greens. Radishes planted near onions often draw the maggots away from onion plants.

Tiny whitish insects, onion thrips, pierce the leaves of onions and suck out the juices. Malathion is the chemical control for onion thrips.

Fungus disease is the most common infection of onions. Rotating crops and planting onions in a soil with good drainage will help to prevent mildew and fungus rots.

Appendix A
Seed To Harvest Calendar

	Start From Seed	Transplant Seedlings	Harvest
JAN	broccoli (I)		broccoli
	cabbage (I)		Brussels sprouts
	cauliflower (I)		cabbage
	lettuce (I)		carrots
	peppers (I)		rutabaga
	tomatoes (I)		turnips
	beets		
	carrots		
	peas		
	radishes		
FEB	eggplant (I)	broccoli	Brussels sprouts
	peppers (I)	cabbage	cabbage
	tomatoes (I)	cauliflower	carrots
		lettuce	cauliflower
	beets	onions	lettuce
	carrots		rutabaga
	chard		turnips
	collards		
	kale		
	kohlrabi		
	mustard		
	peas		
	potatoes		
	radishes		
	rutabaga		
	spinach		
MAR	beets	eggplant	broccoli
	carrots	peppers	lettuce
	chard	tomatoes	onions (green)
	lettuce		peas
	onions		spinach
	parsnips		
	potatoes		
	radishes		
APR	beans	eggplant	broccoli
	beets	peppers	cabbage
	carrots	tomatoes	cauliflower
	corn		fava beans
	cucumbers		lettuce
	melons		onions (green)
	squash		radishes

	Start From Seed	Transplant Seedlings	Harvest
MAY	beans corn cucumbers melons okra pumpkins squash	eggplant peppers tomatoes	beets broccoli cabbage carrots chard lettuce peas radishes tomatoes
JUNE	beans corn melons okra onions pumpkins squash		beans beets carrots chard onions potatoes tomatoes
JULY	broccoli (S) Brussels sprouts (S) cabbage (S) carrots (S) cauliflower (S) potatoes rutabaga		beans beets carrots chard corn cucumbers eggplant okra onions peppers potatoes squash tomatoes
AUG	beets cabbage carrots kohlrabi lettuce peas spinach turnips	broccoli Brussels sprouts cabbage cauliflower	beans beets carrots chard corn cucumbers eggplant okra onions peppers squash tomatoes

	Start From Seed	**Transplant Seedlings**	**Harvest**
SEPT	lettuce radishes rutabaga turnips	broccoli Brussels sprouts cauliflower	carrots chard corn cucumbers eggplant okra peppers pumpkins squash tomatoes
OCT	beets chard fava beans garlic peas radishes spinach	broccoli cauliflower	carrots chard corn eggplant peppers pumpkins squash tomatoes
NOV	chard fava beans garlic onions peas spinach	broccoli cauliflower	beets broccoli cauliflower kohlrabi lettuce peppers potatoes radishes squash tomatoes turnips
DEC	broccoli (I) cabbage (I) cauliflower (I) lettuce (I) garlic onions peas		beets broccoli Brussels sprouts cabbage carrots kohlrabi lettuce radishes turnips

* I: start seeds indoors or in a greenhouse
* S: plant seeds under a shade cloth

This calender is designed for gardeners in California's inland valleys. Foothill gardeners, push back spring planting dates by one month, or plant after the average last frost date in Appendix B.

Appendix B: Average And Record Frost Dates

	Average date of last frost	Record date of last frost	Average date of first frost	Record date of first frost
Auburn	1-21	4-13	12-19	11-14
Berkeley	*	1-19	*	12-26
Burbank	*	3-15	*	11-20
Chico	3-2	4-23	11-30	10-30
Colusa	1-29	4-18	12-4	11-2
Davis	1-19	4-18	12-16	11-2
Lindsay	2-7	4-10	12-4	11-5
Livermore	2-27	4-27	12-2	11-3
Lodi	2-9	3-31	11-30	11-2
Marysville	1-5	3-16	12-21	11-14
Napa	2-9	4-28	12-12	11-9
Nevada City	4-28	6-4	11-4	9-24
Pasadena	*	2-3	*	12-13
Petaluma	2-9	4-29	12-8	11-5
Placerville	4-1	5-18	11-21	10-22
Redding	1-15	4-5	12-17	11-6
Richmond	*	2-13	*	12-15
Riverside	1-14	3-28	1-17	11-12
Sacramento	1-27	3-27	12-10	11-4
San Bernardino	1-16	3-30	1-7	11-14
San Jose	1-24	4-6	12-13	11-10
Santa Ana	*	2-24	*	12-15
Santa Monica	*	*	*	*
Torrance	*	2-11	*	12-8
Visalia	1-17	3-17	12-19	11-8
Woodland	1-27	4-1	12-17	11-5
Yreka	5-14	6-22	10-14	9-14

Frosts do not occur every year.

from: Climatography of the U.S. #20- National Oceanic and Atmospheric Administration.

Appendix C: Elevation And Normal Temperatures

	elev.	JAN	FEB	MAR	APR	MAY	JUN	JLY	AUG	SEP	OCT	NOV	DEC
Auburn	1292	53	58	61	67	76	85	93	92	87	76	63	55
Bakersfield	475	57	63	68	75	83	92	98	96	90	81	67	57
Berkeley	345	56	59	61	63	66	69	69	69	71	69	62	57
Chico	205	53	59	64	71	80	89	95	93	89	78	63	54
Fairfield	38	55	61	65	70	77	83	88	87	86	78	65	56
Fresno	328	54	61	66	73	82	91	97	95	90	79	65	54
Livermore	490	57	61	64	70	76	83	90	89	86	78	66	57
Los Angeles	257	66	68	68	70	73	77	83	84	83	78	72	68
Marysville	60	53	60	66	73	81	89	96	94	89	79	64	54
Napa	60	57	62	65	69	75	80	82	81	82	77	66	58
Nevada City	2520	48	52	55	62	71	80	88	87	80	69	56	50
Oakland	6	54	58	60	62	65	68	70	71	72	69	61	55
Petaluma	16	56	61	63	67	72	78	82	82	82	76	65	57
Placerville	1890	51	55	58	64	73	83	91	90	84	73	59	52
Redding	470	55	61	66	73	83	91	99	97	91	79	64	56
Redwood City	31	58	62	65	70	75	80	82	82	81	74	65	58
Richmond	55	57	61	63	66	68	70	69	70	73	72	64	58
Riverside	840	66	68	70	74	79	86	94	93	90	82	73	67
Sacramento	17	53	60	65	71	79	87	93	91	87	78	64	54
San Diego	13	65	66	65	67	68	71	75	77	76	74	69	66
San Francisco	8	55	59	60	63	66	69	71	71	73	70	62	56
San Jose	67	57	61	64	68	73	78	81	81	80	74	65	58
San Rafael	40	57	62	65	69	74	78	82	81	82	76	65	58
Santa Monica	15	64	63	63	63	64	67	70	72	72	70	68	65
Yreka	2625	43	50	55	62	72	80	90	88	82	69	53	41

from: Climatography of the U.S. #81- National Oceanic and Atmospheric Administration

Appendix D: University Of California Cooperative Extension County Offices

Alameda	(415) 670-5200	Placer	(916) 823-4581
Amador	(209) 223-6482	Plumas-Sierra	(916) 283-0250
Butte	(916) 538-7201	Riverside	(714) 683-6491
Calaveras	(209) 754-4160	Sacramento	(916) 366-2013
Colusa	(916) 458-2105	San Benito	(408) 637-5346
Contra Costa	(415) 646-6540	San Bernardino	(714) 389-2171
Del Norte	(707) 464-4711	San Diego	(619) 565-5376
El Dorado	(916) 626-2468	San Francisco	(415) 586-4115
Fresno	(209) 488-3285	San Joaquin	(209) 944-3711
Glenn	(916) 865-4487	San Luis Obispo	(805) 549-5940
Humboldt	(707) 445-7351	San Mateo	(415) 726-9059
Imperial	(619) 339-4250	Santa Barbara	(805) 968-2149
Inyo-Mono	(619) 873-5891	Santa Clara	(408) 299-2635
Kern	(805) 861-2631	Santa Cruz	(408) 761-4056
Lake	(707) 263-2281	Shasta	(916) 225-5621
Lassen	(916) 257-8311	Siskiyou	(916) 842-2711
Los Angeles	(213) 744-4852	Solano	(707) 429-6381
Madera	(209) 675-7879	Sonoma	(707) 527-2621
Marin	(415) 499-6352	Stanislaus	(209) 571-6654
Mariposa	(209) 966-2417	Sutter-Yuba	(916) 741-7515
Mendocino	(707) 468-4495	Tehama	(916) 527-3101
Merced	(209) 385-7403	Trinity	(916) 628-5495
Modoc	(916) 233-3939	Tulare	(209) 733-6363
Monterey	(408) 758-4637	Tuolomne	(209) 533-5695
Napa	(707) 253-4221	Ventura	(805) 654-2924
Nevada	(916) 273-4563	Yolo	(916) 666-8143
Orange	(714) 774-7050		

INDEX

Aphids 27
Bacillus thuringiensis 26
Beans 83
Beetles 26
Beets 107
Blood meal 16
Bone meal 16
Broccoli 45
Brussels sprouts 45
Cabbage 45
Cabbage worms 26
Carrots 101
Cauliflower 45
Chard, Swiss 107
Chives 131
Collards 45
Compost 16
Companion planting 10
Container gardening 35
Corn 91
Corn earworm 92
Crop rotation 9
Crop selection 5
Cucumbers 75
Cutworms 26
Diazinon 27
Diseases 24
Double digging 18
Drainage 13
Eggplant 65
Fertilizer 15
Garden journal 10
Garlic 131
Hardpan 15
Harvest 136
Insects 25
Intercropping 9
Jerusalem artichokes 72
Kale 45
Kohlrabi 45
Leafhopper 26
Leaf miner 26
Leeks 131
Lettuce 119
Light 3, 35
Malathion 27
Melons 75
Mulches 15
Mustard greens 45

Nitrogen 18
Okra 97
Onions 131
Organic soil amendments 16
Parsnips 101
Peanuts 87
Peas 125
Peppers 51
Pests 25
Phosphorus 18
Planning 1
Planting 8
Potassium 18
Potatoes 69
Pumpkins 75
Pyrethrum 27
Radicchio 122
Radishes 113
Raised beds 18
Relays 9
Rotenone 27
Rutabaga 45
Seed catalogs 7
Seeds 8
Sevin 27
Shallots 131
Soil 4, 13
Soil pH 18
Soil structure and texture 13
Spider mites 29
Spinach 107
Squash 75
Succession planting 9
Sunlight 3, 35
Swiss chard 107
Tomatoes 57
Transplanting 33
Turnips 45
Watering 4
Watermelons 78
Weeds 21
Whiteflies 26
Windowsill garden 115

About The Author

Marsha Prillwitz is:

A University of California Master Gardener

A garden writer for the Sacramento Bee since 1980

A California gardener for almost 20 years